The CashPT® Blueprint

How I Built and Scaled a Successful
Cash-Based Physical Therapy Practice
Even When I Was Told It Was Unethical,
a Bad Idea and That No One Would Pay
More Than Their Copay for Physical Therapy!

AARON LEBAUER

Copyright © 2019 Aaron LeBauer.

All rights reserved. No part of this book may be reproduced, stored, or transmitted by any means—whether auditory, graphic, mechanical, or electronic—without written permission of the author, except in the case of brief excerpts used in critical articles and reviews. Unauthorized reproduction of any part of this work is illegal and is punishable by law.

This book is a work of non-fiction. Unless otherwise noted, the author and the publisher make no explicit guarantees as to the accuracy of the information contained in this book and in some cases, names of people and places have been altered to protect their privacy.

ISBN: 978-1-6847-0278-7 (sc)
ISBN: 978-1-6847-0277-0 (e)

Because of the dynamic nature of the Internet, any web addresses or links contained in this book may have changed since publication and may no longer be valid. The views expressed in this work are solely those of the author and do not necessarily reflect the views of the publisher, and the publisher hereby disclaims any responsibility for them.

Any people depicted in stock imagery provided by Getty Images are models, and such images are being used for illustrative purposes only. Certain stock imagery © Getty Images.

Lulu Publishing Services rev. date: 08/27/2019

To my wife, Andra, for encouraging me to become a physical therapist and supporting me unconditionally, even when my ideas seem a bit crazy.

To my father, Joe LeBauer, for instilling in me the importance of doing what's right for patients, no matter what. Without his influence you wouldn't even be holding this book.

Contents

The CashPT® Manifesto viii
My CashPT® Story xi

Part 1—The CashPT® Blueprint

Chapter 1   The Anatomy of a Cash-Based Practice 1
Chapter 2   The CashPT® Mindset 5
Chapter 3   Aaron LeBauer's Practice Blueprint 12
Chapter 4   Transitioning to A Cash-Based Practice 24
Chapter 5   Cash & Compliance 28

Part 2—The CashPT® Marketing System

Chapter 6   USP 43
Chapter 7   Getting New Patients 47
Chapter 8   The Real Problem is Not Marketing 56
Chapter 9   Online Marketing 62
Chapter 10 Lead Generation Systems 70

Part 3—The Entrepreneur Mindset

Chapter 11 Entrepreneur Mindset..77

Appendix 91
The CashPT® Checklist 92
Daily Success Checklist..95
"Do You Take My Insurance?" Call Script 99
Thank You Note Script 103
Patient Re-Activation Email Script 105
List of Local Fitness and Health Professionals to Contact...... 107
Sample Superbill 109
Notes 111
Acknowledgements...117
About the Author 119

The CashPT® Manifesto

My name is Aaron LeBauer,

And I'm part of a select group of Physical Therapy Entrepreneurs who many people think are crazy.

We don't count on referrals from physicians and our goals are to never rely on insurance for reimbursement...

In fact, our goal is much different.

You see, we have an opportunity to transform people's lives because we are fighting against insurance companies—the establishment who only care about their investors.

We have to do things differently. We have to do things better, smarter and with more compassion.

We don't rely on insurance companies for reimbursement because it limits how we treat patients.

We don't beg for referrals from physicians because we are Doctors of Physical Therapy.

We have to run a successful practice from day one.

How is this even possible?

If you ask your teachers and clinical instructors, they will tell you what we are doing is crazy, stupid or will never work...

But it's happening all over the world.

It's happening is this business model we call CashPT®.

It's something I can't really explain to you; it's something you have to see for yourself.

There are thousands of passionate physical therapists just like you doing this every day and making it work.

We use the CashPT® model to make our dreams a reality.

We work for patients *not* insurance companies...

We are CashPT®.

My CashPT® Story

Where do we start? I suppose it's 1973. My name is Aaron and I'm a Sagittarius.

I was born in Greensboro, North Carolina to a medical family. I've lived in both California and North Carolina during my lifetime. I've got a beautiful family. I've got an awesome, supportive wife and two daughters who wake us up every morning before we're supposed to be getting up, but then don't want to get out the door for school.

I co-own LeBauer Physical Therapy here in Greensboro with my wife. Our practice is 100% cash-based and is almost 100% Direct Access.

I went to Duke University thinking I was going to be pre-med. Being a physician was what I felt like I needed to do. My dad, uncles, grandfather and great-uncle were all physicians and becoming one too was not only expected of me, but it was really the only thing I knew to be successful.

But then my first day in organic chemistry came along and I couldn't complete the homework. Well, I knew I could complete it, but it was going to take me four hours and I sat there going back and forth like, *is this going to be my life?* From then on, I was no longer a pre-med student. I told myself I was going to take classes that I enjoyed, hang out with my friends, ride bikes, play sports and build a life that was fun.

After I graduated from Duke University, I spent a year learning and volunteering in Israel. Upon my return, I moved out to California with my best friend, Eric. We had spent a summer living in Berkeley together and knew that's where we needed to be to start our lives.

I didn't want to get just any old job; I wanted to find one that matched my values. I worked for months to get an interview at some of my favorite brands, all companies that focused on outdoors and the lifestyle that I wanted. I finally landed an interview at Sports Street Marketing, the makers of Gu Energy Gel. I wore a suit to the interview, because that's just what you did when you grow up in NC and go to Duke, and they were like, "We don't dress that formally here." It was California, remember. I was like, "Oh, I know you're supposed to wear a suit to job interviews." They looked at me like I was crazy.

After getting turned down for the job, my next interview was at Sierra Designs for a customer service position. I wore a sweater. I did get a second interview, but not the job. Eric was a temp making $14/hour and it was good money, so he got me my first gig stuffing envelopes. I did the temp thing for a while. People treated me like I didn't have an education or even knew the alphabet. I got a job to go to a company and help them organize their filing system and my "boss" went through the whole alphabet with me, like there was a good chance I didn't actually know it. On another job, which was a sweet gig, I was the "fax boy." I delivered faxes and in my spare time sent letters to drum up sponsorship for my cycling team. After about five weeks, my supervisor invited me to lunch because she had exciting news for me. She offered me a job as the new mail clerk when my peers were on the floor trading millions of dollars. I said to the woman, "Look, I graduated from college. I can do exactly what these guys do. Thank you but this isn't why I'm here."

On my next job, I was working for some insurance underwriters on the 43rd floor of Embarcadero 4 (there were five Embarcadero Center buildings, all 40 stories or more). They tried to get me to train their staff on a new computer program. I asked for a raise. Long story short, I only got an extra $0.50 to train their permanent staff, all the while the college interns were getting the red carpet.

One day I was hiding out—I had finished my work too fast—and saw all the bike messengers riding around downtown, getting paid for doing something I loved. So, the next day, I went to the largest bike messenger outfit and signed up. I had raced bikes in college, and since moving to San Francisco, didn't have the time or money to get back into racing. Racing bikes was actually how I first got introduced to the benefits of massage therapy. I had gone to get a massage when I was struggling with my training and it changed how I felt on the bike tremendously. So, massage therapy was in the back of my mind for a career path, but never really a reality because it wasn't up to the standards of being a "doctor."

One day, after a long day on the bike—typically eight hours and 100+ miles—I wondered, "How am I going to do the things I want to do?" I was in the shower, and it just hit me: I could become a massage therapist, treat four or five people a day, and have 19 more hours in the day to do all the other stuff that I wanted to do out of life. I would have the time and money to start racing bikes again.

I made the decision to go to massage therapy school at The National Holistic Institute in Emeryville, CA. It's sandwiched between Berkeley and the Bay Bridge. While there, I was able to race again and start a career that I was meant for. It was a career where I could help people who were in pain, who had been let down by the system and who had nowhere else to turn.

I raced bikes seriously for about eight years and became a Category 1 cyclist, the top amateur level in the country. I raced all over the U.S. and in Europe. My best sponsors were Visa and MasterCard. I finished my bike riding career with over $40K in credit card debt, but it was 100% worth it.

I pushed myself as hard as I could, got further than I ever imagined and missed out on a professional contract just because I was 28 years old and not 26. I climbed off my bike in 2004 because I had nothing left to race for and wanted nothing more than to spend my time with my girlfriend, now wife, Andra. The big lesson here is to push yourself, go all in, and when you exceed your goals, set bigger ones. Even when you have been let down or "seemingly" fail, there is always a lesson to be learned and growth on the horizon.

Working in California as a massage therapist was unique. For instance, everyone knew that when you get hurt or you tweak something, you go see your massage therapist. At the time, there was no Direct Access to physical therapy, and patients needed to wait weeks to get in to see their physician before being referred. So, people were coming to see me for that purpose. These were folks who had already been to PT and Chiropractic, those who had surgery and weren't getting better. The big thing that was missing from their care was the hands-on soft tissue treatment that they needed. I had started studying myofascial release after I graduated from massage school and the new techniques I was using were helping my patients. I was told, "No one's been able to touch me where it hurt, find 'the spot' or even give me any relief until I started working with you."

My wife Andra has been instrumental in this whole journey. She is the one who pushed me to go to PT school, inspired me to work hard to become a better person and who has stood beside me when things in the business seemed like it was going to shit. She has been the biggest source of strength and inspiration for me and the person I've leaned on to get through the tough patches. She's also been the source of many great ideas that sometimes seem like they are my own, but in reality, have been planted carefully by her. We met in San Francisco, both massage therapists, both having been to the same massage school the same year, but never met until years later.

Let's get back to my journey from massage therapy to physical therapy. It seemed like a logical progression, but not one, living in California, that I needed to make to help people. I was already charging $80 per hour with a growing practice in San Francisco. However, Andra had been pushing me to go back to school and get a degree as a physical therapist because she saw something in me that she believed people needed.

As a talented massage therapist herself, she knew I would be able to help people even more. At the time, living in San Francisco, there were no physical therapy programs I could attend without moving out of town and that were not going to require that I take an additional two years of school getting my pre-requisites.

We moved from San Francisco, not because we didn't love it, but because we didn't see a future for us there. We moved to be near her family in San Luis Obispo, CA. After living in San Luis Obispo for 10 months, we knew we had to leave. I had only seen five patients in my practice the whole 10 months! We each had the best job possible as massage therapists at the premier spa in the region, Sycamore Mineral Springs. Our friends were 15 years younger or 15 years older since it's a college town or retirement location and we were in our early 30's. We couldn't see ourselves growing there or still able to afford to buy a home.

So, instead of moving to LA or back to San Francisco (or throwing a dart at the map), we decided to give North Carolina a try. I grew up in Greensboro, NC and we were interested in the potential opportunity to move somewhere cool like Chapel Hill or Asheville where we could also afford to buy a home and grow our family. Within six months of moving to Greensboro, we were engaged, excited new home owners and both enrolled back in school.

I went to an open house at Elon University to check out their Doctor of Physical Therapy program. At the time, they had rolling admissions and told me there were only two spots left. I signed up for the GRE that day, took it that Saturday, got the score I needed by one question and finished up the second of two pre-requisites I needed. It was one of the best decisions I've ever made.

I started my 100% cash practice right after graduating from Elon University's DPT program. I have never worked for another physical therapy clinic, hospital or health care company as a physical therapist since. I realized long ago, while working as a temp on the 43rd floor, that I hate being micromanaged and thrive when given the freedom to do things my way, not the way I'm expected to do it.

I help active people who want to stay fit, healthy and mobile without medications, injections or surgery. Those are my patients. Most of them have back pain. Most of them have chronic pain and unresolved pain and I see plenty of people with hip, knee, neck, foot, ankle, jaw, pretty much everything. Even weird things that you wouldn't think PT or hands-on can help. Maybe it helps, maybe it doesn't, but if I can get in and reassure someone that their problem isn't the end of the world, that helps tremendously. To have someone sit and listen to them, even if I can't physically change what's happening, people love that. People don't get it anywhere else, especially in the current model.

Let me ask you a question: What's the greatest number of patients you've treated in one day? I bet you can't guess mine. I treated 43 patients one day as a student. 43 patients! On my *first* clinical rotation. Think about that for a minute.

That's more than four people per hour for a 10-hour workday. That was the day that I decided I wouldn't do insurance-based PT.

There were some naysayers and people that didn't believe in me. I had a clinical instructor who I told about my plans to open a cash practice, and he looked at me and said, "That's not going to work. No one is going to pay more than their copay for physical therapy." I looked at him and I was like, "Well, let's check in in three years and then we'll talk about that then." I haven't heard from him since...

When I was graduating, most of the instructors asked something like, "So Aaron, where did you get a job? Where are you going to work?" And my typical response was, "LeBauer Physical Therapy." They'd look at me and go, "What do you mean?" or give some crazy expression of surprise. I would say, "Well, I'm starting my own practice," and they'd reply, "Oh wow. Do you have all the insurance stuff set up?" When I told them I wasn't taking insurance, they looked at me with a blank stare like I was crazy. Pretty much anyone I told said I had to take insurance. I even heard from people that it was illegal *not* to take insurance.

Here's the thing: I had maintained my massage therapy practice while I was in school seeing five to eight clients a week and was already earning $85 per hour for a therapeutic massage. Once I started looking at potential jobs as a physical therapist, I quickly realized that the only jobs available paid $35-40/hour and no one was going to hire me, even at that amount, to treat patients the way I thought they should be treated. Shoot, insurance companies were sure not to reimburse my treatments of primarily one-on-one manual therapy because they don't value this type of service or healing. I remember, at the time, United Health Care had announced that they were only going to pay $45 per physical therapy visit no matter what was provided. It's the reason I sold my UHC stock, which was a gift from my father and at the time was valued at approximately $24/share. It's now, at the time of this writing, worth over $270 per share. I couldn't live with myself owning a share in that company, and even today, I would rather not have the earnings these shares would have generated for me because I don't align with their purpose once so ever.

I also knew that I worked best in an environment where I could make decisions and be autonomous. There really was no job opportunity in Greensboro where I was going to be an autonomous provider and be able to make decisions independently for my patients. This, along with the fact that insurance was going to try and dictate treatment, lead me to believe that all I had to do was start offering "physical therapy" instead of "massage therapy" and I could charge $10 more per visit.

On my last clinical rotation at Physical Therapy Innovations in El Cerrito, CA, my CI and now close friend, Allen Ling, supported me in building my cash practice. He helped teach me what was working in his business and I learned first-hand what did not. Most importantly, he gave me his support and helped me focus my six months on not just clinical but learning the business side. He assigned me a project of creating a business plan to present to him. It was non-traditional plan, basically a PowerPoint presentation, because I was not seeking financing, just organizing my ideas. I did all this and was ready to leave and get started, but then Allen turned around an offered me an amazing job and compensation package larger than any of my classmates. I was already the only one getting a stipend plus housing and I had to turn down this amazing opportunity to return to the Bay Area, the part of the country I fell in love with 15 years prior.

Once I started telling other physical therapists about my plans to open a clinic and do it without taking insurance, I had a lot of resistance. Back then, in 2009, there was no CashPT®. People didn't talk about "cash-based physical therapy," but they certainly understood that creating a PT clinic without filing insurance was suicide.

Along with Allan, I had the support of my family, my wife and my father the cardiologist, who despite encouraging me early on to leverage our connections in the medical community, has been one of our top referral sources and the only physician to refer more than two or three patients. My father, Joe, was the one who always instilled in me from a young age that it's important to do what's right for your patients above all else.

Even with their support, in the beginning they still didn't have much hope. However, I knew in my heart that what I was doing was the right thing for my patients, my sanity and my family. We started in a small two-room office in a nondescript building in downtown Greensboro. We were in the same office for over seven years before moving to our current location.

After a few years of proving that a purely out-of-network physical therapy practice, one that marketed direct to patients and not to physicians, actually did work, I was just cruising along, treating 20+ patients a week, spending Monday and Friday afternoons with my kids and Tuesday and Thursday mornings working out, riding my bike or practicing yoga. Things were going great, but my brain thrives on excitement and stimulation and I was looking for something else.

I found myself helping other people do the same thing for their practice by answering questions from classmates, in online forums, blogs and social media. I created a free Facebook group, The CashPT® Nation, to help inspire others to feel confident and part of a community on their own journey.

I started writing on my own blog, hosting free webinars and launched a podcast called The CashPT® Lunch Hour to share the answers to people's common questions and dispel some of the myths and false beliefs. I believe that it's really important to have mentors to learn (and in return, show others) what is possible when you take a leap of faith, when you have an idea and you put it forward.

I have since taught over 500 passionate physical therapists how to start, grow and scale their cash-based practice through my flagship course, The CashPT® Blueprint, and have helped inspire 1,000's of others to go out on their own and achieve their dreams through my blog, podcast, Facebook group, free webinars and working with my Platinum Mastermind group during our monthly calls and our live events three times a year. I get messages every day about how others have been inspired by something I've said or written. I've realized through this whole process that I have much more to give than just helping one patient at a time. I have the opportunity to help so many more people beyond just the ones I meet in person. By sharing my experiences, knowledge and proven strategies with other physical therapy entrepreneurs, who in turn, can help patients in their community, I can have a much greater impact on the world.

My goal in this book and in life is to empower other passionate physical therapists just like you to create, grow and market a successful cash-based practice even when you've been told it won't work, is a bad idea and no one will pay more than their copay for physical therapy.

After five years of grinding and about a year of coasting, I decided that to regain the free time I had lost to starting a coaching business and to truly make an impact in my local community, I needed to hire another physical therapist and to grow and scale our practice.

This wasn't possible without having seen other people do the same or similar.

To achieve massive success, you need to expose yourself to the success of others. As my mentor and business coach, Bedros, says, "success leaves clues." In just a few years, I was able to pick up on a lot of them.

During one of my trips to expose myself to other people, I attended Lewis Howes' Summit of Greatness. Lewis is another one of my coaches and business mentors, and after sitting through half a dozen talks by world-renowned motivational speakers, I realized a few things they all had in common. First, they all used about 10 or less presentation slides. Second, they had a vision or mission in their life that was much bigger than them.

It took me a few days to process this and another few months to really connect with my why and my own mission:

I am on a mission to save 100 million people worldwide from unnecessary surgery.

Why is this my mission? Because I've sat through countless evaluations with patients who have told me they were frustrated, upset or just at their wit's end as to why they continue to hurt. Then, after my evaluation, and even just speaking to them, realize they've never been to see a physical therapist, or if they have, they were not touched.

I find that I'm able to touch them somewhere no one else has, or even just give them hope and encouragement that's been missing in their care. I've grown tired and even frustrated myself and some days feel like I'm going to bash my head against the wall if I hear another story about how "my doctor told me I didn't need physical therapy" or "I think I need an MRI to know what's going on with my back."

I'm sure you've heard a variation of the same.

It was my patient, "Steve," who I saw who really pushed me over the edge. He had come in to see me as a last-ditch hope. He was being told he needed yet another ankle surgery to remove the scar tissue that was causing his pain.

It started with a sprained ankle that didn't get better with rest, bracing and pain medication. Nothing showed up on the X-Ray or MRI so a surgery was performed to "see what was going on." Apparently, there were no fractures or damaged tissue… until after the surgery! Then, when his pain and symptoms didn't resolve after another six months, he underwent a second surgery to clean out his ankle from the scar tissue that was a result of the first surgery.

Along the way he was given opioid pain medications and by the time he was sitting in front of me in my office, he was a self-professed opioid addict. He wanted to get off of them, but the pain clinic didn't give him a plan to do this, they only treated him "like a criminal." Steve traveled frequently for work and if he was going to be out of town when his 30-day supply was set to run out, he was unable to refill it beforehand and if he ran out while on the other side of the country, he would have a few miserable days of pain and withdrawal symptoms. Then, upon his return, he would go in to get a refill from the pain clinic and feel like they treated him like an addict. All the while, all he wanted was to get off the meds and for the pain to ease up a bit.

He was never *once* recommended to see a physical therapist or rehab professional.

Another story is about a local physician with whom I had spoken with a few times about our mutual patients. He was one of the few local MD's who would actually answer the phone when I called and passed along compliments he heard from patients he had seen that had been to our office.

The tragic part of the tale is that he passed away as a result of spinal surgery. I don't know any of the details. I don't know why the surgery was indicated or not, all I do know is that even when he complimented us on our care for back pain, we never saw him in our office before I read the obituary in the paper.

Preventing more stories like this are why I stay up late and work hard to spread the message of marketing direct to patients and creating a business that serves patients first. I can't make a significant impact alone and need your help in the fight. Most people think "the physical therapy" is the same everywhere and they do not realize that there are many variations and many different physical therapists who might offer a different opinion, and it's your job to do everything you can to let the public know how you can help.

As of this writing, LeBauer Physical Therapy employs two physical therapists, one massage therapist and a customer care specialist. My wife and I still work in the business, but our primary role is managing our employees and growing the clinic while also taking care of our own bodies and spending time with our daughters. We're not the first to scale a cash practice and we will not be the last. One of the big goals I set a few years ago when I was planning to hire another therapist was to have financial freedom and location independence when our daughters go off to college since we would like to be able to live somewhere else for a month at a time or more. We actually already have that, but since our kids are still in school, we'll just have to settle for a few weeks at a time each summer.

Our plan is to grow our clinic so that we are the primary care provider for pain and musculoskeletal injuries and patients know they need to call us first. We will help 10,000 people in Greensboro over the next decade avoid unnecessary medications, imaging, surgery and recover from painful conditions and injuries so they can be active, fit, healthy and mobile.

PART 1

The CashPT® Blueprint

Frustrated with insurance companies dictating your treatments and withholding payments?

Overwhelmed by starting a cash-based therapy practice and unsure where to turn for help?

Eager to transition your current in-network practice to a cash-based practice?

Do you want a simple system for starting a cash-based therapy practice?

In the follow chapters you are going to get the step-by-step template to start a cash-based practice from scratch that over 500 successful cash-based physical therapists have used to build their own thriving physical therapy businesses. These important lessons are distilled down from over 20 years of trial and error in my own businesses and all you have to do is choose to believe it's possible for you too.

Chapter 1

The Anatomy of a Cash-Based Practice

We're going to start by covering the anatomy of my practice. Why an overview of my practice? Well, to show you what is possible for yours. You may not have or want the same type of practice that I have. You may have an idea for something completely different, like a home health-based mobile practice, working in pediatrics, a gym-based practice, an online business or something entirely different. Just understanding, knowing and seeing what other people are doing can help you create the practice of your dreams.

Sometimes it's hard to imagine what's possible, or even believe it can become true, until you've seen it for yourself.

This is also important because I want to demonstrate to you how a low overhead cash-based practice can operate successfully and be scaled to multiple therapists so you can earn a great income, even while on vacation.

OUR PATIENTS

We have a low overhead practice. We maintain a small footprint. We don't use any equipment or modalities in our practice, so we don't have anything that's expensive to maintain or to buy or purchase. We generally see one patient every hour.

We provide almost all hands-on therapy using myofascial release, manual physical therapy, craniosacral therapy, soft tissue mobilization, deep tissue massage, trigger point therapy, trigger point dry needling, taping and most importantly, we teach and empower our patients to treat themselves at home using a lot of the same techniques.

When we see a patient for the first time, one of the biggest things that we do is to spend time talking to them. We let them tell their story.

Our patients in general have chronic pain or unresolved pain. They've been around the block, been to see other therapists, chiropractors, massage therapists, physicians, surgeons, etc. They've been on pain medications, had injections and even surgery, and are still struggling with their pain, symptoms and inability to return to their "normal" lifestyle. They're looking for something else, something other than the cookie cutter treatment they've received elsewhere. They don't want hot packs, leg lifts or ultrasound. They don't want to ride a bike for 10 minutes. They don't want to do exercises "they already know how to do" or "can do on their own at their gym."

They're looking for a new path. They want something more. Our patients are people who value their health, who are active or want to be active again and who want to improve their current condition so they can focus on what they value most. They want to participate in their own healing process.

CLINIC ENVIRONMENT

When it comes to your treatment room, keeping it simple is my best advice. Whether you're using equipment or not, ask yourself, "Do I really need this to provide the best treatment possible for my patients? Do I really need 3,000 square feet of treatment space? Do I really need to lease that $75,000 AlterG anti-gravity treadmill?" As you plan your practice, start to consider these things.

Overall, just make sure to provide your patients with a comfortable therapeutic environment. We have soft music playing, as well as dim lighting to make the experience more relaxing. We also provide water to them, which I think is a must.

This is much different than your busy open gym treatment area or style found in many orthopedic clinics. I believe our way is more healing and supportive based on my experience as a massage therapist and what hundreds of patients have reported to me over the years.

Finally, we sell self-treatment tools in our waiting area. These are the tools that we use personally, and which help support the manual therapy interventions we provide in the clinic. We don't count on the revenue from these, nor can we get great margins. I think this is important since our patients can walk out the door with the recommended product right away and start using it to get better.

STARTUP COSTS

I started by depositing $10,000 into my new business bank account. This covered all my equipment, rent and marketing materials. A big chunk of it was estimated living expenses for the first few months until I had some cash flow. I know a former practice owner who started their own clinic with just $500 in the bank and years later, after a lot of hard work and success, sold it for a multiple six or seven figure sum.

When I started, I already owned a portable massage table, an expense that's well worth it if you are doing any manual techniques. Budget about $900 to $1,000 on a quality American made portable massage table. I have to say, the quality of table makes a huge difference. The higher quality tables last a lot longer. Stay away from the cheap Costco or Amazon special. You can often find high quality used tables on Craigslist or Facebook.

In our first clinic location, we were paying $300 in rent a month, which is really inexpensive. We didn't have a very big space, just two rooms and a closet large enough for a desk. One was the waiting room/office and the other was the treatment room. It was far from prime real estate and that doesn't really matter. If you have a strong value proposition, patients will come to you. We've had patients drive an hour and come as far as California to be treated in our clinic.

Chapter 2

The CashPT® Mindset

One of the most important things you need to be successful in this practice model is the cash-based mindset. You may already have it, but you definitely weren't taught it in PT school. If you're reading this book, you probably have it, but we just need to bring it to the surface. What is it, you may ask? *The idea that we are worth much more than a "copay."*

In this chapter, we're going to talk about the different mindsets you should have in the cash-based model. If you're not a physical therapist, I want you to understand that a lot of these ideas are going to apply to your profession or situation whether it's occupational therapy, massage therapy, chiropractic, etc. The ideas in this book are based on solid, longstanding, foundational business principles that we'll dive deep into in later chapters.

THE WORTH MINDSET

One of the things I want you to think about right now is how much you paid for your degree. How much is that worth?

Now, think about the last patient who told you "you changed my life" or "you gave me my life back." How about the patient who you saved from back surgery? Or from getting a double hip replacement at 45 years old? Or having their foot amputated because of chronic pain from a possible hospital-borne infection? Or even death on the operating table? What is that worth to them?

How much do you need to earn each month to sustain yourself, and how much do you need to earn to make a good living? The next step is to say to yourself in a mirror, "I charge X per hour." There's a lot of self-doubt here but practicing it will help you grow confidence in your worth.

I can't tell you exactly what you should charge, but if you're charging less than the typical copay, the Medicare allowable, less than your dentist charges you for a teeth cleaning or basing your rates on what your colleagues are charging, you need to rethink your pricing strategies.

The likelihood is that you're afraid to charge more because it feels unethical to sell physical therapy and you're afraid of being perceived as sleazy. This is very common and understandable. You were never taught your worth and value to your patients. This is what a majority of my students struggle with, something I worked hard to overcome. Once I figured out the secret to ethically selling physical therapy it transformed our business. You are worth so much more than just a copay, so don't settle there. This struggle is what I teach people how to overcome and why I created my course, Ethical Influence.

THE VALUE MINDSET

You have to lead with value and provide value to your patients. You also need to value yourself.

What is value? Value is what you provide to your patients so that they know and understand you will help them get what they want. You give them value by asking the right questions and helping them get the transformation they deserve.

Patients don't want more knee range of motion or even to be pain free. They want to be able to finally complete the 5K, get a PR in CrossFit, play with their kids on the floor, dance at their daughter's wedding and feel strong and independent so they can run away if they have to.

Valuing ourselves is rather tricky, because it's not something you were taught in PT school, in your clinical rotations or even in your last job. You are valuable to patients because of how you transform their lives. You value also includes your expertise, your skills and your education.

So, to show your value as a business, consider what can you provide that is unique. In a cash-based model, we're almost always seeing one person at a time, and we have the freedom to spend as much time or as little time as we need with them, so we can spend 30 minutes, but a lot of people are going to spend 45, 60, even 90 minutes with their patients one-on-one. Just having the time to sit and listen to their story. That's valuable in and of itself. What other expertise and skills do you have that can't be provided in an in-network or contractual setting or that no one else in your town is able to provide? What questions can you ask them that will help your patient understand what they truly want and how you can help? That's where you can really show value to your patients.

A lot of times patients will call and find out how much we charge and say, "Okay, I need to use my in-network," and a few months later they'll call back because they were unsatisfied with their care elsewhere.

Money or price is never the objection. The objection is always around a lack of clarity and understanding of value. Yes, patients will pay hundreds, even thousands, to see you for physical therapy if they understand and value what it is that you offer and how you will help them make the transformation they desire and get the results that they want.

Yes, patients will pay for physical therapy. No, not all patients will pay. There are a lot of people who feel like they need to use their benefits, but it's not even that they need to. They just don't understand the difference between what we can offer one day a week versus what someone else offers three days a week.

Patients will forgo their excellent insurance benefits and pay hundreds of dollars per visit if *you* know exactly what *they* want and desire and *why* it's so important to them to get it.

THE PRIMARY CARE PHYSICAL THERAPY MINDSET

If I view myself as a primary care physical therapist, I am the person that people come to see first when they hurt or have trouble moving. We are the point of entry into healthcare. We are referring patients to physicians and other providers. I now have the power as the referral source and position as the expert on movement disorders and musculoskeletal dysfunction.

Direct Access for physical therapy means that patients do not need to have a referral script or a prescription for physical therapy to see a physical therapist. This is a state by state, profession by profession issue.

Marketing directly to patients is part of claiming, owning and taking responsibility for Direct Access. The patients are our customer, not physicians or insurance companies. The patients are the ones who will ultimately make the decision to see you, or not. We need to focus our marketing directly to our potential patients' needs, wants and desires and get out of the mindset of, "Oh, I need to market to physicians. I need a physician's referral to see or treat a patient."

Even if your state only has Direct Access to evaluation, you can evaluate them and make a recommendation for their plan of care. Then, based on your specific practice act, you contact their physician or the last healthcare provider that can refer to you or write the necessary "script." Sometimes it can even be a dentist or provider in another state. You make it part of the onboarding process to get what the patient needs to be seen in your clinic. There are ways to work with these limitations and stay within the law, and we (physical therapists) need to start operating from the place where we are the person that this patient can see first. This is who you are going to market your services to and that's where together we are going to focus our efforts.

Aaron LeBauer

THE "DOCTOR" MINDSET

This is soapbox topic for me, so get ready!

Who is a doctor anyways? In physical therapy, we have somewhat of an identity crisis.

"I *need* a physician referral." That statement *needs* to go in the trash, because in 50 states, we do not need a physician's referral for evaluation or even to speak with a patient on the phone and ask them a few simple, yet very important questions.

Patients are typically not ready to "buy in" to our physical therapy plan of care when they come to our clinic if referred from a physician. Patients are not really expecting anything different. "So, I went to see my physician, the godlike person, and I only paid $50 or even $25 to see them. Why am I going to pay you, a physical therapy technician, more?"

If I ask, "What did your doctor say?" when speaking to patients, then I'm totally devaluing my degree and my position of authority as a healthcare provider and an expert in musculoskeletal care. Instead I will ask, "What did your physician say about that? What did your physician recommend?"

Who are you? I told you who I am. Who are you?

Write it down. Say it in the mirror. Say it 100 times. A primary care physical therapist.

"I am Dr. LeBauer, and I am your physical therapist."

I am positioning myself in that statement mentally, physically and emotionally as the primary point of care for people who have pain, injuries and limited motion. It is a mindset, an expectation, a way of being.

This is not for people who have blood squirting out or bones sticking out of their arm, but people that hurt, people that can't move very well, people who think they just need an MRI to "know what's going on." I am the primary point of contact for them and I am the musculoskeletal expert. I am the doctor.

Chapter 3

Aaron LeBauer's Practice Blueprint

In this chapter, I will outline the logistical steps you need to take to open the doors to your practice and see your first patient. We will talk about the nitty gritty of opening a practice, from the permits to what happens if a patient no-shows.

Your success is a matter of intention. It's no longer a question of "will a cash practice work?" The question now is: "Is a cash-based practice right for me?" We've come to the point where this is a proven model no matter where you live or who your patient population is. It's not for only wealthy people or large cities. Those are just myths and excuses for not wanting to do the hard work. Being willing to go down the less trodden path and determination to do the hard work is all you need. If you put out to the world your intention, say that you're going to open a cash-based clinic and that it is going to be successful, it is going to create your success.

LICENSES AND PERMITS

One of the first things you'll need is a city or state license to practice physical therapy. You'll also likely need a business license. In my state in North Carolina, the business license for physical therapy practices is a statewide license called the Art of Healing License, and it's the same license that's required by massage therapists, physicians and occupational therapists. Since it is a statewide license, I do not need a city business license to practice physical therapy. Every state is different, and the likelihood that your city or state will have a different scenario, is high, but the circumstances may be very similar. It may be called something different. You may have to have a license to practice physical therapy as well as a city or state business license and it's up to you to do that research.

If you are going to sell tangible items or taxable items, you will likely need a sales tax license or resellers license. If you have a brick and mortar clinic, you may also need a building permit, inspection and other documentation to create a business and this is going to be location specific as well.

This may especially apply if you change anything to your office suite or build something new like a sign, an office build out, bathroom and doorway renovations to comply with the Americans with Disabilities Act, and many more. Finally, don't forget about signage permits for shopping centers or neighborhoods.

The first major thing you need in place before you treat a patient is personal and business liability insurance. This protects you and your assets. You will also need general liability, and this protects your company. This is going to be a different policy than the liability insurance you have just working as an employee.

Next, you will need to form a business entity. There are a couple of different options for this step. The easiest and least expensive way to start out is with a sole proprietorship. As an individual therapist, as a sole practitioner, you are your business. This is the least expensive route, but it also affords you the least protections. The next option, single member LLC, doesn't hide who you are to the public and costs a bit more. This option to form a corporation is still the best one, and there are a lot of options depending on where you live as the type of entity you can form is determined by your state's practice act. Be sure you consult with your lawyer and accountant before deciding which corporate entity you will create.

Finally, you will need an NPI number or National Provider Identifier. You likely already have one if you've been employed as a physical therapist or own an in-network provider and you're transitioning to a cash practice. If you already have a personal NPI and work somewhere else, just go get a Type 2 NPI for your business once you file your corporate entity and have a new business EIN.

I didn't start with an NPI, as it's actually not required by law to have one. Patients were still able to receive reimbursement even though I did not have an NPI number. It doesn't need to be the first on your list, but it should be something that you're thinking about or putting on the back burner because you will be asked for it at some point. For the five minutes it takes to obtain, it's worth reducing the hassle of not having it in the future.

While we're on the topic of professional advice, I would strongly encourage you to consider consulting with a lawyer versed in healthcare or business, especially when it comes time to create your consent to treat, privacy statements and legal documentation. Do this right the first time, so when you are busy later on you don't have to waste time fixing it. Take it from me and learn from my mistakes.

LOCATION

Location, location, location.

If your service is unique, people will be willing to travel to see you. The whole "location" thing is important and in a niche business it doesn't matter really where you are located as long as it's safe, has easy parking and your patients can get to your office. People who value your service and understand that what you do is different will be willing to go pretty much anywhere to see you. They will go into any building and travel to any town.

There are a lot of cash-based practices I know—mine included—where people will travel an hour or two or more to come in based on a recommendation or internet search because something is not available in their area. We have a patient that flies across the country to see us. She found us on YouTube and has a daughter that lives 90 minutes away. She comes in to town to see her daughter and schedules two-three visits with us each time.

The other consideration for where to locate your clinic is the demographics of your perfect patient. Where are the population centers? Where do people live?

We started in downtown Greensboro, and the reason I really liked this location was not because of its proximity to wealthy people or the fancy shopping center. I chose this location because it was easily accessible from the highway and all neighborhoods in town while also being a nice location that was affordable for our projected revenue.

Important considerations for choosing a location for your practice:

- Is the street safe at night?
- How will winter weather affect it?
- Do I want signage? And walk in traffic?
- Do I want to have a standalone office building?
- Do I want to have an office suite?
- Do I want to rent a room from another therapy practice or sublease within another facility?

One more very important thing: take into consideration if someone in pain, using a wheelchair or has difficulty walking will be able to get into your office. Is there a wheelchair ramp if necessary? Are you on the second story with no elevator?

You have your location, so you'll have a physical address. Sometimes when you sublease, use multiple locations or have a MobilePT practice, you'll need a business mailing address. Go to a UPS store and rent a P.O. box. When you use UPS, you'll have a physical address instead of a "P.O. box" number, which looks more professional.

If you're subleasing space, be sure that part of your agreement is that you can receive mail, set up your own internet and have access to utilities or can set up your own. Most importantly, you want your phone number answered by someone who is trained to speak to your patients in the correct way and who knows how to answer the ever-important question, "Do you take my insurance?"

PAYMENT

When it comes to payment, accept all major credit cards and be done with it. I've seen a lot of resistance from people through posts online about accepting credit cards and if they can charge patients the fee. Here's the deal: if the credit card fee seems like a lot, you are not charging enough. Just raise your rates an extra five bucks and it will not be an issue.

When choosing a merchant card processor, look for a company that will easily allow you to accept same day payments, set up payment plans and even keep the card number (or unique token number) on file to make it easy for your customers to do business with you. These features will come in handy later, so you have options when asking patients for payment. You'll also want to choose a merchant processor who will deposit your money in your account within 24 hours and even has an option for a mobile card reader.

When it comes to discounts, you may feel compelled to offer them, especially when you're first starting out with the hope of getting more people in the door. You are not competing with the in-network clinic down the street, so stop thinking that you need to be priced similarly.

Discounts should not be used to get people in the door. They should be used, if you are going to use them at all, to get patients to commit to your recommended plan of care. When I've offered discounts in the past, it didn't get more people in the door, and the people who came in only wanted the discount. They did not value what I was offering at the full price. If I offered or gave away a free treatment, all they wanted was the free visit, and they took a lot of time trying to get more "free" advice. When you offer a free visit or consultation, you need to be sure you pre-frame the offer and carefully screen the prospects so that only the right patients are able to claim a free visit.

ACCOUNTING

So, how should you keep track of your income and expenses? The easiest and cheapest way to do this is to go buy a little paper ledger from an office supply store and make a column for expenses and a column for income. At the end of the year, add it all up and give it to your accountant.

What we currently use is QuickBooks Desktop Pro. It can be used on a Mac or a PC and there are quite a few options these days online. The desktop version, you pay once, and it's good until you get rid of your computer. The drawback of using QuickBooks is that if you ever get audited by the IRS, they can have access to all of your past records because they are all part of the same file. This is one of the reasons I have hired a bookkeeper to do my monthly record keeping and accounting.

The other benefit for me using a bookkeeper is that it saves me time manually entering in my receipts and expenses or doing my own payroll. My bookkeeper has saved me tens of thousands by helping me strategize my investments and restructure my business organization so that I am paying myself a salary with my taxes and retirement savings coming out before the money hits my personal bank account.

Now, as a private practice business owner, you have to pay your own taxes. This may or may not come as a surprise to you, but if you are not paying yourself as an employee of your own business yet, plan on paying estimated taxes once a quarter. Plan on putting aside about 30% of your generated revenue into another account. Yes, it's a significant hit, but that's what we get for doing business for ourselves. It's totally worth it. Check in with your accountant and find out from them what's a good amount to start prepaying. You don't have to pay it quarterly, but when they do your taxes at the end of the tax year in March, you will likely have quite a hefty tax bill for the previous year if you haven't prepaid. Don't ask me how I know....

SUPERBILLS & RECEIPTS

I provide all of my patients with receipts or a "super bill" that is customized using QuickBooks—another reason I use this software. You can use a paper print-out like I include in The CashPT® Toolkit or utilize bills for your patients. The superbill we give out to patients contains all of the information they need to submit their own claim to their insurance company. I include their ICD-9 diagnosis code(s) and CPT treatment codes along with all of my practice information, a signature and tax id number or EIN.

A superbill does not guarantee your patients will get reimbursed and the promise to get reimbursed should never be the reason a patient chooses your practice. Patients are directed to contact their insurance company to obtain the form which they should fill out to submit a self-claim. We'll instruct our patients to be sure to let their insurance company know that they have already paid for the services and that the reimbursement should be sent directly to them. Sometimes all the patient will need to do is send in the receipts we provide. People who have Health Savings or Flex Spending Accounts can pay with their HSA or FSA credit cards or check books. We let our patients know that we are happy to answer any of their questions and will provide any documentation they need directly to them (our patient) if their insurance company makes this request.

We also include a bold ted line on the superbill stating: **"The patient has paid for the service provided in full and LeBauer Physical Therapy is NOT an insurance provider for this claim. Please provide payment directly to the patient."** Occasionally, we will still receive a reimbursement check made out to the practice or a request for our tax ID number.

I've included a sample superbill in the appendix of this book for you to reference. If you're looking for more documentation to use in your practice, check out The CashPT® Toolkit → AaronLeBauer.com/Toolkit.

CANCELATION POLICY

This is another major policy that you need to have in place before you start seeing your first patient. It needs to be clear to the patients ahead of time. In order for it to be clear to your patients, it needs to be clear to you. It will only work when it is enforced, so you have to enforce it. You have to have your policy and you have to stand by it.

We have a 24-hour cancellation policy. If the patient questions why, explain you have the policy in place because you only see one person at a time. If the patient cancels or no-shows past that time period, we charge them 100% of the session cost. That being said, the first time it happens, we usually let it go and inform them of the infraction in a nice way. We say, "Mrs. Jones, we understand life is messy, so the first one is on us." If it becomes a recurring thing, we will charge them. It's only fair to you and your other patients.

"DO YOU TAKE MY INSURANCE?"

Now, this is the age-old question and number one objection you will hear. When someone asks, "do you take my insurance?" they're asking you to say yes or no. Instead of saying no, we have another way to explain it.

You want to start with connecting with your patient. You need to redirect the conversation because often they don't know what else to ask and have been trained by typical medical offices that asking about 'insurance' is an important first question. Think back to the last time you called to make an appointment with a medical provider! Did they ask your name and inquire about what is going on and why it was important for you to call that day? Or were the primary questions "What's your date of birth?" and "What is your insurance?"

It's important to help guide the conversation, to ask engaging questions and show we care primarily about them as a person. We also want to give the patient a few opportunities to say "yes" and to give us permission to explain what we do and how we can help. Asking the right questions is how we show value up front so that when we come to the part of the conversation about insurance or payment, it is secondary to their understanding of our ability to care and nurture them back to health.

One key point here is that when selling a product or service, if someone has already answered "yes" in the conversation about their desires and needs, they are much more likely to say "yes" to your offer in the end.

It's also important to reassure them that they have called the right place and that you treat this condition every day.

Some great questions to ask in the call are as follows:

"What are you unable to do because of this problem? Or, what are you unable to do as well as you would like because of this problem?"

"Has something changed recently that you've now decided you need to look for a different solution or alternative?"

"Mrs. Jones imagine if we were having this conversation again in three months, even a year from now. Looking back over that time, what has to happen for you to feel happy with your progress and that working with us was the best decision you ever made?"

If you're looking for the full call script, check it out in the appendix of this book!

Once you frame to the patient what they are investing in, when they ask again about insurance, tell them that almost all of your patients have great insurance and that your clinic is out of network.

One thing you need to learn is to be okay with people who are not ready yet. Give up the need to please or treat everybody. There is no way that Aaron LeBauer can treat everyone, and neither can you.

HOW TO FIND OUT MORE?

I've created a free CashPT® Checklist for you that contains every step you need to take to start your cash-based physical therapy practice. It's the same checklist I used when I started plus the new steps I've discovered along the way.

I've included it in the appendix of this book, and you can also go here to download it for FREE → AaronLeBauer.com/Checklist

Chapter 4

Transitioning to A Cash-Based Practice

This chapter is primarily for the "in-network" practice owner that is frustrated with losing money treating patients or just tired of the fight for reimbursement. It is absolutely okay to be in-network with some insurance companies, especially if they are low hassle and still pay well.

Before making a commitment to transitioning completely or partially to the cash-based model, you should consider your current practice philosophy. Will that fit with a cash-based practice? Do you have a niche? Do you have a service that is unique to your area?

Think about your overhead and financial commitments because those are going to change. Are you currently renting really expensive equipment or really expensive office space? Your needs may change, cashflow my change and patient volume *will* change. If you are currently seeing multiple patients an hour, it is highly likely that your patient volume will change as you have more time to spend with each patient and less pressure to stack patients to generate revenue.

"Will my current patients stay?" This is the number one question and fear I hear from people who are in an in-network clinic and thinking about transitioning to a cash-based clinic. No, not all patients are going to stay with you. That's okay. The number one thing you can do is help them find another quality therapist in your town.

As you move into a higher value service, people may not want that and that's okay. We have to give that up because patients will come. The other thing you can do to create an added benefit for some of these patients that may not stay is to file on behalf of your patients, especially if you already have the infrastructure set up to do that. Whether that's through an online EMR, billing company or in-house billing assistance.

If you already have these systems in place, then you're really just becoming an "out-of-network" clinic. Patients still pay you in full, but they don't have to do the intimidating legwork.

When it comes to making the leap, do you transition gradually, or cold turkey? I recommend more of a gradual approach, but if you're fed up and you've got the volume and people coming in already, you may as well start from the top and work your way down. You may not need to wait long to start dropping your contracts.

You need to know both your value and your cost to provide a service to your patients. Your value is what you bring to the table, and your cost is your expenses divided by your total treatments or treatment hours. A lot of people don't know their cost to provide a service. I once asked this question in a room full of business owners and therapists, and a dozen hands went up. People didn't know their cost to provide physical therapy per hour or per patient visit. You need to know this, because if your cost to treat is more than your contracted rate, you are losing money! I just spoke with a therapist on the phone recently and after 10 years her cost to treat a patient is $64.65/visit and her average reimbursement was $58.76! You do the math on that one...

Start by dropping the lowest paying contracts and/or the contracts that are the hardest to collect. Start prioritizing your schedule and changing the way you onboard your patients so you can have the appropriate conversation with them, so they don't care if you "take their insurance" or not. Then you'll have a winning formula and a robust and profitable practice without the headaches or influence on how you treat your patients.

ADDING CASH-BASED SERVICES

Instead of just dropping insurance contracts, you can start to add cash-based services like massage therapy to transition your patient population. Think of it this way: the insurance-based treatments are the reason customers walk in the door, the cash-based services such as massage, yoga, Pilates, gym memberships, nutrition, health coaching, etc. are the back-end upsell. This is where you'll generate a nice profit in your business while adding significant value to your customer's experience.

For instance, you can utilize massage therapists to do some more hands-on soft tissue work and spend more time with patients after you've treated them. It can be a cash-based addition to their physical therapy, where after the course of their physical therapy, people can come in for somewhat regular massage therapy treatments.

Group classes are also a great way to offer cash-based services. If you get 10 people into a group class for $35 dollars a person, you're making $350 dollars for the 45 or 60-minute class. A yoga or Pilates physical therapist-led exercise type of class is highly valuable. People with injuries or recovering from injuries can come and feel safe and you charge $25 or $50 dollars a person. If you pack the room full, you could make quite a bit of money for your time, while delivering an affordable and highly sought-after experience.

There are some physical therapy businesses that only have corporate accounts. These are still "cash-based" because there is not third-party payor. You can save corporations millions of dollars working in corporate accounts where you, or someone on your staff, come in once a month or once a week for an hour or two and see people that are not "injured," but have been identified or self-selected as needing some help. See them for 10-15 minutes each and maybe see eight to 10 people in two hours. In this way you can save the corporations a lot of money on workers compensation claims. That is a whole separate course, and it's a great addition to your cash-based services.

Chapter 5

Cash & Compliance

Now it's time to talk about the nitty gritty: compliance in your cash practice. Why is this so important?

Just because you now accept "cash" payments from your patients does not mean that there are no rules to follow and you do not need to comply with state and federal regulations. A clear understanding of the rules and having consent and patient agreements in place will help minimize your risk and exposure to liability claims. Your patients need to have a clear understanding of the services you are providing and their financial responsibility.

INFORMED CONSENT

First off, let me state that I am not a lawyer and the following should not be considered legal advice. You should consult with a healthcare attorney and your state's practice act to be sure that you are operating within both your state and federal laws.

Let's start with informed consent. This is a process for getting permission before conducting a health care intervention on a person. This is the consent patients give to receive treatment and hands-on therapy. Your payment policy can also be included in this consent form. Our informed consent and payment policy blend together. We also have a consent for photographs and testimonials that patients provide. Informed consent can also include an acknowledgement that patients have been provided with your privacy statement.

DEFENSIBLE DOCUMENTATION

Myth: In a cash practice, I don't need to worry about my documentation.

False. You still need to pay attention to your documentation. If you are not a Medicare provider, you do not need to document to Medicare standards, and if you are not contracted with an insurance company, you do not need to document to their standards. You *do* need to follow your state's practice act guidelines for documentation, and you should document to CYA: Cover Your Ass.

Medical records will be requested by private insurance, by legal counsel and with liability claims. A majority of the time, they just want to confirm that the patient was actually seen and treated in your clinic. In my experience they are not really scrutinizing your treatment so much, however there is the possibility that they will request your records and even bring you in to court to talk about your records as a witness. However unlikely it is, you need to CYA.

You also need to document so that *you* know what to do next. Document for yourself, to help your treatments and patients improve, and document to make sure that other people can understand and read your documentation. Let go of how you've learned to document and do it with your patient in mind, not the insurance companies' requirements that you are used to. In our practice, using G Suite for business takes about two minutes to document a patient note and five for an evaluation.

Another common question is: "Do I need to show medical necessity?"

No. You actually don't, because you are not documenting for your patient's insurance company, you are documenting for your patient. *We work FOR our patients, NOT insurance companies,* so if the insurance company is going to deny a claim based on your documentation because you were doing the best thing for your patient, that should not be your concern. It is not something that you need to be overly worried about; it's an issue between your patient and their insurance company.

You do not need to document to try to make sure that patients get paid or reimbursed. Unfortunately, these days deductibles are so high that patients are not really getting reimbursed anyway. Document for yourself, so you know what happened, and document to make sure that people can read your notes and understand what you did in the clinic.

HIPAA

I receive quite a few questions regarding compliance issues when discussing the cash-based physical therapy practice model. These include Medicare, HIPAA, patient privacy, documentation, Direct Access, multiple services and more. In general, it would seem like these issues should apply to a cash-based practice in the same manner as a traditional insurance-based practice, but the details might surprise you. There is a lot of misinformation and misunderstanding floating around, especially regarding HIPAA and putting its rules and regulations into practice, including the assumption that we are all "covered."

My curiosity started when my brother, who is in private practice as a social worker counseling individuals and couples, first brought a HIPAA compliance issue to my attention. He forwarded to me an email correspondence written by a lawyer, who is an advisor to another therapist in my brother's mental health therapist network. I have not been in personal contact with this lawyer, but the email I received stated that his opinion is "anyone who does NOT do electronic billing, remove the HIPAA forms from their intake packets. If you include HIPAA forms, you are subject to HIPAA rules and regulations and if you violate any of those you can be strictly fined."

This really got me thinking and asking myself questions. When I set up my practice in 2009, I was told I needed to have my patients sign a HIPAA privacy release form. Upon hearing this new information, I was now concerned that doing so might unnecessarily jeopardize or put my practice at risk. This deserved some more investigation and in researching this, I've learned quite a bit, though not all the answers. I want to share what I've learned.

HIPAA is the Health Insurance Portability and Accountability Act of 1996 and it was primarily aimed at providing workers with easier ways to continue their healthcare insurance coverage whenever they changed jobs.

An area of special consideration was the transfer or portability of patient records. The easiest way to make data transfers is electronically and the most common is via email. Unfortunately, email is not a secure form of communication. Legislators added appropriate language to ensure the confidentiality of patient information when stored or sent electronically, which became the first legislation to address email confidentiality. HIPAA is about patient confidentiality in electronic format.

The first question to ask yourself is: "Is my practice a covered entity?"

The CMS website has an excellent flow sheet to help you answer this question and determine if you are a covered entity.

The Administrative Simplification standards adopted by Health and Human Services (HHS) under HIPAA apply to any entity that is:

- a health care provider that conducts certain standard transactions in electronic form (called here a "covered health care provider")
- a health care clearinghouse
- a health plan

Another typical question is: "What are the 'certain standard transactions?'"

Transactions are electronic exchanges involving the transfer of information between two parties for specific purposes. For example, a health care provider will send a claim to a health plan to request payment for medical services.

Data sent by email and through the Internet, even if scanned into a pdf file, is an electronic transmission. Another interpretation of this is that if the data or information originates on a computer (including a cell phone or tablet), it is an electronic transmission.

There are two aspects to determining if you are a "covered entity" or not: the purpose of the transaction and how it is delivered. Certain Standard Transactions include Protected Health Information and if you send or transmit any of these transactions electronically, you are a covered entity.

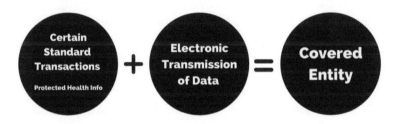

Even if you are not a covered entity under those circumstances, you still have to conform to the standards of practice and privacy ethics as outlined in your state's practice act and/or your professional association.

My practice does not fit the definition of a covered entity. HIPAA consent forms are no longer something I have my patients sign.

Instead, I have my patients sign an informed consent form that includes the following statement:

"I understand that LeBauer Physical Therapy, LLC will maintain my privacy to the highest standards and may use or disclose my personal health information for the purposes of carrying out treatment, obtaining payment, evaluating the quality of services provided and any administrative operations related to treatment or payment."

Likewise, just as my documentation is the same as if I owned a traditional insurance-based practice, I protect my patients' privacy when in public, in my office and on social media. I also keep a standard landline and use a traditional fax machine the two-three times a year I am requested to send patient information.

If you have a 100% cash-based practice, you are likely not participating in any of the "certain standard transactions" anyway. If you want to maintain a simple and low-key existence and avoid being a HIPAA covered entity, or even the gray areas and uncertainty in the middle, be sure you communicate via phone, snail mail or standard fax. Remember if you hire someone else to do this for you, or on your behalf, be sure they do the same and insist that health plans and insurance companies communicate with you only via phone, snail mail or standard fax.

Just to be clear, this is really best left for you and your healthcare attorney to decide based on your unique practice, federal and state regulations. When I was first aware of this issue, I looked at the HIPAA regulations and rules posted on the CMS website and discovered that I was not a covered entity based on their algorithm. Recently, after extensive conversations with my healthcare attorney, she pointed out that there are two HIPAA rules: the Security Rule and the Privacy Rule. She said the "non-covered entity" status I mention in this chapter applies to the Security Rule, and that everyone is bound to the Privacy Rule. Her advice to me was to be sure and sign a BAA with Google since I use G-Suite and IntakeQ. However, I'm also still using an analog fax and not sending patient notes to the insurance companies when they request it. I send the notes directly to our patient. She also recommended that I have patients sign that they've been provided a copy of our HIPAA notice of privacy practices and post this notice on our website. That way we are complying with the Privacy Rule and still not bound by the Security Rule. This just shows how complex these issues are and why it's best to have a great lawyer (or two) on your team.

MEDICARE

Well, this has been a long time coming. It's the elephant in the room, Big Brother, a.k.a. Medicare. The relationship dynamic between Medicare and physical therapists is a tough one to navigate, considering all of the compliance and payment issues, it is difficult on a good day. Add in a dose of cash-based physical therapy and you have a recipe for muddy water that you might not want to drink.

I am going to describe my experience with running a cash-based physical therapy practice and not being enrolled with Medicare.

Medicare typically sets the standard for what most private third-party insurance companies implement. Thankfully, while some are still in the dark ages, most third-party payors will honor Direct Access reimbursement to their insured beneficiaries. I live in North Carolina, and I am lucky that I have very favorable Direct Access laws. I rarely receive a physician's referral and most of my patients do not have a prescription. I have not had a patient tell me they were denied because of a lack of a physician's referral, script or prescription for physical therapy.

Unfortunately, this is not how it works with Medicare. Every Medicare beneficiary needs a prescription from their physician and a signed plan of care to receive somewhat limited physical therapy benefits. Medicare rules require that Medicare Beneficiaries only receive treatment for "covered services" from Medicare providers. There is a limit on the amount of services they can receive unless the patient has specific needs required beyond typical "covered services" and then modifiers are needed.

When starting my practice, I chose not to become an in-network provider or enroll with Medicare so that I can provide high quality one-on-one hands-on care to patients for as long as I deem necessary. The big problem is that I am now very limited in who, what and how I can treat the huge and rising Baby Boomer population.

As I was writing my business plan, I had no clue there would be an issue with Medicare. I assumed that everyone in the United States had the right to choose their healthcare provider. I first learned this might be an issue when searching for information on how to file an Advanced Beneficiary Notice (ABN). I was incorrectly advised by another therapist that I needed my Medicare patients to sign an ABN so I could treat them in my practice.

In my search to find out what needed to be on an ABN, I started to realize the reality of the situation: most people have no clue what the rules are or what they are talking about, even the local APTA

Medicare advisor had the wrong information when I contacted them back in 2009.

As a physical therapist in private practice you have three choices regarding a relationship with Medicare.

1. Enroll and participate (PAR)
2. Enroll and not participate (NON-PAR)
3. Have no relationship with Medicare (My status)

You can choose your Medicare arrangement and provide cash-based services to patients who are not Medicare beneficiaries. In options one and two, you can provide treatment to any Medicare beneficiary and you must document and maintain compliance as per Medicare regulations. It is only option three, no relationship with Medicare, where you cannot treat Medicare beneficiaries for "covered services."

When I was a Licensed Massage and Bodywork Therapist in North Carolina and in California, I could treat whoever I wanted. I just could not manipulate a joint or provide a medical diagnosis. Now that I am practicing as a physical therapist in North Carolina, I cannot manipulate the spine without a physician's order (NC law) and I cannot treat Medicare beneficiaries without a physician's referral. Furthermore, in my cash-based practice where I am not a Medicare provider, I cannot treat Medicare patients for "covered services."

The deeper problem was that no one I spoke to really seemed to know the rules. Every time I asked or inquired, I would come away with a different answer. I was basically told by one person, who was the state level reimbursement specialist, that I am not allowed to *not* be enrolled as a Medicare provider and if I am not enrolled, I basically can't even breathe near a Medicare beneficiary until I am. Even the APTA Medicare advisor could not give me a black and white definitive answer on who I could treat and for what. It seemed the more questions I asked the more restricted I felt, and the more people turned their attention to me to say "no."

Fortunately, reality and the truth are often misunderstood. There are some instances where it is totally appropriate and legal for a Medicare beneficiary to be seen by a physical therapist who is not enrolled as a Medicare provider.

As the Medicare specialist in North Carolina basically told me, "Aaron, you can't so much as breathe on a Medicare patient, no matter what you're doing, even if it's out in public." He was like, "You have to be enrolled. It's the law." It is not the law that you have to be enrolled in Medicare. Most people think that they only need an ABN, and the patient signs it, and they're good. That's not true, either.

The ABN is only a document you give to patients if you are enrolled in Medicare and are providing services that are not covered by Medicare, typically for something like dry needling or when the beneficiary has met or exceeded their cap. I'm not and have never been a Medicare provider and if you are, please discuss this with your compliance team, consultant or healthcare lawyer.

Confused yet? No worries. That's normal. As you can see, there are a lot of extensive and intricate legal regulations on taking private-payment from Medicare beneficiaries, regardless of the type of service or the type of physical therapy practice, and the above information doesn't even scratch the surface!

Before you make a decision about treating Medicare beneficiaries or not, or who you can treat in your practice and how, you should definitely learn everything you can about the subject (I have hours of training and resources in my online course) and be sure you consult with a healthcare attorney about your options and for help creating your consent and payment agreements.

For more in-depth information about Medicare and HIPAA check out these posts on my blog here → AaronLeBauer.com/Medicare

PART 2

The CashPT® Marketing System

In the following chapters, you will learn the exact marketing strategies and systems that I've put into place in our clinic and taught to thousands of successful cash practice owners. These exact systems and strategies are what we use to consistently get new patients calling our practice every day to schedule an appointment for physical therapy. They are exactly what allow me to go on vacation and continue to generate revenue. These systems have given me the freedom to spend more time treating patients, more time with my family and more time working "on" my business, rather than always hustling and sitting around waiting for the next person to call.

These are not difficult, they just take work to install. The truth is, most people don't want to put in the hard work. But once you put in the work to install these systems into your business, all you'll have to do is occasionally "turn a dial" and you can almost predict how many new people will call the next week. My first CashPT® Resident, Dr. Derek Nielsen from Kaizen Physical Therapy in Durham, NC, always reminds me that I never actually "did any marketing" the whole 13 months he worked here in our clinic. Yet, his schedule was always full. That was only possible because of the robust marketing systems I put in place after I figured out the secret formula I'm about to share with you...

Chapter 6

USP

Before you start marketing your clinic, you need to have a clear understanding of who you are talking to, who your perfect patient is and what you help them do. It's not enough to just say, "We're great so choose us" or "the physical therapy you deserve." No one really understands what "physical therapy" is. They think it's just post-surgical rehab, hot packs, leg lifts and ultrasound, time on an exercise bike or exercises they already know how to do at home.

If you market to everyone, you market to no one. The riches are in the niches, so we need to be specific and create a marketing message that speaks to your perfect patient. You need to put yourself in their shoes and ask, "What's in it for me?" Think about what your patients want to hear so that their thought process is, "That's exactly my problem" and "She totally gets me." To do this we need to create a marketing message that is about the patients, describes exactly who you can help and the transformation you can help them achieve. Once you've established your Unique Serving/Selling/Value Proposition (USP or UVP) and know exactly who your perfect patient or avatar is, then you can use all the marketing ideas and strategies in this book to target the specific people in your community who are most likely to become your patient.

So, what is a USP or UVP? It's not your slogan or catchphrase. It's a clear statement that describes the benefits of your offer, how you solve your customers' needs, and what distinguishes you from the competition.

While you may have spent countless hours and hundreds of thousands of dollars on your degree and credentials, patients don't care. They want to know what's in it for them. The alphabet soup of credentials behind your name, your certifications in a specific type of treatment and your accomplishments in our field are not what they want to know or how they will decide to choose you as their physical therapist.

Your USP is almost like your elevator pitch: it's how you can explain what you do in plain language in less than a minute. It's something real humans are supposed to understand. It's for people to read. This should not be technical language; it shouldn't be physical therapy language—it should be the language of your patients. It should be the language of your perfect patient.

Here's mine:

At LeBauer Physical Therapy, we help active people in Greensboro, NC stay fit, healthy and mobile without pain medications, injections or surgery.

Why did I choose this USP? A lot of my patients who've come in over the years have told me they chose us because they want to avoid getting surgery, they don't like being on the medications or they've tried the medications and injections and surgery and it hasn't worked. I help them stay healthy and fit and recover from their past injuries, and most of those people are people who are active, want to be active, were active or are interested in actively participating in their health. Choose a USP that describes who you've been most successful helping or who you love working with.

Here are some words I would caution you guys *not* to use: "we help people eliminate pain" or "we help people get rid of pain." When you're doing that, you're promising the end of pain.

Ending pain isn't always something that's a winning result. A lot of people can get back to running a 5K and they're still going to have pain. We're supposed to have pain. Pain is a natural response of the body to a threatening stimulus. It's important and part of life.

I recommend leaving "pain" out of the conversation, but "pain medications" can totally be part of it.

Here's the USP formula:

"We help _____*describe who*__ do ____*this, that and the other thing*___ without this_*thing they want to avoid*___."

Or, "_____*describe who*__ do ____*this, that and the other thing*___ with ____*result they really want*____."

So, where do you display your USP? Put it on your website, your business cards and your promotional materials. Put it on your self-treatment tools. Even use it as front signage. Your USP is much more important than your company logo, so make sure it gets prime real estate.

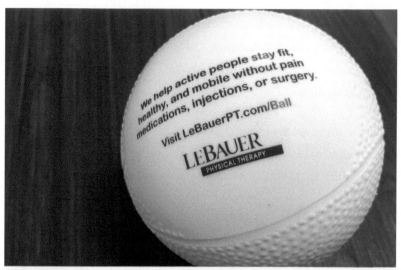

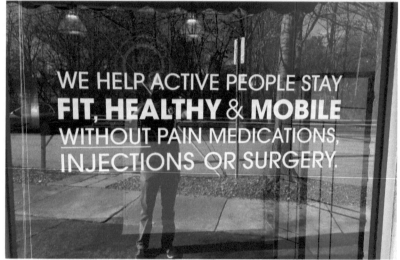

Chapter 7

Getting New Patients

Let's dive into my top seven strategies to getting new patients in your clinic.

FREE TOTAL BODY DIAGNOSTIC

This is a free 20-minute visit. It's actually not a marketing strategy as much as a sales strategy. This is especially important if you are charging higher prices or have patients who are unaware of exactly what you can do and how you can help. It's not a treatment session. It is a free consultation, but by calling it Total Body Diagnostic Testing (TBD), it describes a little bit better what we're doing for them.

Think of the TBD like a cheaper, easier and more accurate alternative to an MRI. As physical therapists we know that MRI's are sensitive, but not specific, meaning that even patients without pain will have "positive" findings on an MRI. MRI's are over-utilized, scare patients, lead to more surgeries and cost patients more money in the long run.

One of the most common phrases I hear from potential patients and even existing patients is "I need an MRI to know exactly what's going on." This TBD exam is one of the answers to solving this misconception. It's an opportunity to sit and talk with your potential patient and for you to do a full body diagnostic screen, ask the right questions so you have a clear understanding of what they will need to get better and for your potential patients to discover and understand "exactly what's going on."

Most importantly, it's an opportunity to get to know each other. This is something that is not just for anyone who wants something for free. This is for people who are already looking for a solution to their problem and are just having trouble making a decision or need some more information to be able to make the best decision for themselves or a family member.

They are afraid they might make the wrong decision, because they have likely been let down in the past or made decisions they regretted before. It is an opportunity to come in and window-shop us a little bit.

At the end of a TBD or right before you roll it into a full-price evaluation, you will give the patient a firm diagnosis and a prescription. Always pre-frame or let them know beforehand that this will be an option and schedule them so you have time to roll the TBD over into an evaluation if the patient agrees.

"Mrs. Jones, my recommendation is that we get you started in our Total Body Transformation program. It's just _____ and when you

decide to move forward, we can get started right away teaching you a customized home self-treatment program, creating your personalized plan of care and helping you ___ (restate their vision and goals)___ so you can avoid __ (all the things they don't want to have happen)___. How does that sound?"

MARKETING TO YOUR WARMEST LEADS

It's a myth that as a physical therapist you cannot earn $100,000 per year or more. More importantly as a physical therapy business owner, you do not need more new patients to earn the number. Most business owners are only looking at one statistic: the number of new patients coming through the door. They are only focused on getting more new patients, likely because that's what you've been told you need by lots of savvy marketers out there. They are great marketers, however what you need to do is to increase the lifetime value of your current patients and customers.

It is a proven marketing principle that it's much easier to sell a product or service to someone who is already your customer and made a purchase in the past than to sell to a cold prospect.

Patient reactivation emails are awesome. If you already have a list of former patients and they are no longer coming in to see you right now or they haven't been to see you for weeks, this is an amazing strategy. It works and can help you fill your schedule this week! It is a bulk—though personalized—email check-in to see how they are doing. This simple message can re-activate dozens of patients right now.

Use an email auto-responder program to send out your bulk emails, newsletters, blog post updates, etc. We use Active Campaign to send out broadcast emails to our patients. It's easier than trying to email 100's of people with your personal account and there are no privacy concerns like when you forget to Bcc people and you put all your patients addresses in the CC line instead! Oops!

People will likely reply back, "I've been meaning to get back in touch after my vacation" or "I'm almost there and not doing as well as I thought." This is a perfect opportunity to get them back in for a tune up. They may ask, "My back is great, but my knee is bothering me... do you treat knees?"

On the other hand, maybe you'll get a "Oh, I'm doing great," or "Thanks for checking in." This is a perfect opportunity to ask for a testimonial, an online review or just for them to share their story with their family and friends who may also benefit from physical therapy.

FOLLOW-UP CALLS

This is a follow-up phone call that you can use with past patients too. You can use it for people who have inquired about your services but haven't scheduled. You can use it for people who have dropped off the schedule. You should also follow up with people who you send the re-activation email to from the second strategy and who download your free e-book, gift or inquire about physical therapy from your website or attend one of your in-person workshops. Same thing.

"Hey, Miss Jones, it's Dr. LeBauer from LeBauer Physical Therapy. Do you have a minute to chat today?"

Have a conversation. Ask questions. See if you can help them understand what they are struggling with and why it's important to them. When both you and the patient understand why, then you have a big reason to get them into your clinic.

THE SOCIAL MEDIA SNEAK ATTACK

This is the secret strategy no one is talking about! Go in and post a testimonial of a patient who's given you permission to share it. You can post it on your personal page, Instagram, your business page, etc. Anywhere people will see it and comment. You are giving the patient recognition for doing hard work and getting results. You tag the patient with their permission so it shows up on their wall or on their profile, tag your business and create a call to action at the end for people to comment below.

A second variation is to post an educational video to your business page and then share it on your personal page. Talk about the "what" and "why" but leave the "how to fix it" for when people become your patient.

Once posted, be sure you comment and interact with people and then send a private message to the people who like and comment on the post. The goal is to start a conversation with them and if they seem like they might need some PT, get them on the phone and if they are a good fit, offer a free Total Body Diagnostic Test.

These are people who have already engaged with you. They've liked it, they've commented, and then what you're going to do is say, "Hey, this is Dr. LeBauer. Thank you so much for supporting Mrs. Jones. I really appreciate that." It shows that you really care about her, and you can ask, "Is there anything going on with you that is keeping you from being active the way that you would like?"

You want to get them off Facebook and on the phone. They don't have to be calling you or ready to come in to see you, but if you do this with enough people, you will find people who are struggling to find a solution to their problem.

THE MONSTER FOLLOW-UP

We want to follow up with people in many different ways. For instance, when someone becomes your patient, you want to email them, "Thank you for becoming my patient. Here's your information." That's part of the new patient email sequence. You also want to follow up with them on the phone.

We even want to send people a text if we can't get them on the phone. Many people these days don't answer the phone for numbers they don't recognize, but they will answer a text, even if you are just asking if it's a good time to chat.

"Hey Mrs. Jones, this is Dr. LeBauer. I just sent you an email and left a message on the phone. Just want to know how you're doing. I want to check in since we had a visit yesterday and I thought maybe you might be a little sore. Do you have a few minutes to chat on the phone?"

When you do this follow-up, the idea is that you're going to get a response within 24 hours, and then you can have a conversation, get them on the phone, start talking about their problems and get them scheduled.

GRAND OPENING/RE-OPENING

Most of these strategies so far are perfect if you already have patients and just want more. The grand re-opening is a great strategy if you're new or even if you're 10 years in business and want to scale up.

The first step is finding a local charity whose mission and values align with yours.

Next, you want to put together a drawing. You maybe go out and buy an iPad or another free gift. You can also give away a free Total Body Diagnostic or a self-treatment tool. To be entered, people pay $5. 100% of the money you raise is donated to the charity. You're also going to collect contact information on the entries, so make an entry form with a space for a name, phone number and email.

You are going to call up other businesses who also have the same customer as you and ask them to become a sponsor for your event. Maybe they can help provide or sponsor food, beverages or complementary services. When we did a grand opening, we had one of the local grocery stores give us some appetizers and wine. We had a bike shop send over some drinks and snacks. It was great.

You are going to ask your sponsors to send out a few emails and post on social media helping to promote the event and the drawing. This will not only form close community relationships, but you will be able to leverage their email list, contacts and customers to become your own (and vice versa) by making this about something bigger than just physical therapy.

You want to invite everyone you know and ask them to bring a friend. You will email everyone on your list, everyone on Facebook, invite your friends, create a Facebook event where you share about the event. Ask everyone to share it because you are supporting a higher purpose and giving back to the community.

You should also contact local news outlets, the chamber of commerce, associations, etc. This positions you as an expert and community leader and you will be getting recognition. Give to get! In return, you will build your list of potential patients and people will begin to know how you can help them.

COMMUNITY WORKSHOPS

This is still one of the most powerful marketing strategies and what we consistently go back to whenever we want to turn the dial and generate more new patients. Reach out to local gyms, running stores, yoga studios, social action groups, religious groups, fitness and health related business owners, people you know, etc. See if they are interested in having you create a customized workshop for their community.

You can create a workshop focused on any of your specialties and your perfect patient, however the best thing to do is build rapport and ask if there are any issues their members are struggling with or anything in particular you can help them with so you have relevant needs wants and desires to create a workshop that they want, need and will respond to.

For instance, my current CashPT® Resident, Dr. Tyler Shelton, did a workshop recently on how to safely lift a person off the ground. We actually got paid for it!

We also recently connected with a new local health food restaurant that has had a line out the door since day one and saw they were already doing "pop up" Pilates, Yoga and Boxing sessions on the weekend. I connected with them on Instagram, sent a few messages, and within two weeks we taught a Movement and Mobility workshop there and in within just a week, booked two new patients and have a dozen others to follow up with by phone and email.

At the end of the workshop, make sure to say, "Be sure you to sign in! Just leave me your name, email and phone number and later on today I'm going to send you the handouts and the video that I made that go over everything we did." Boom, dozens of people on your email list. Be sure you follow up with them via email within 24 hours and by phone within 48 hours.

You're promising value so they shouldn't hesitate to give you their contact information!

Get 35 more marketing strategies here →
AaronLeBauer.com/Marketing-Strategies

Chapter 8

The Real Problem is Not Marketing

Marketing is just not enough. You may not even have a marketing problem. A lot of people say to me, "Oh Aaron, I need new patients and I need to do more marketing."

After speaking with them on the phone or during one of my Platinum Mastermind hot-seat sessions and getting a deep look at their business, I'll say, "Well, you don't have the follow up systems (sales and conversions processes) in place for the marketing to actually work."

The big thing I want to leave you with is, yes, marketing is great. Marketing like paid Facebook advertising is awesome and sexy. It's *the thing* everyone gets excited about, but if you don't have the follow-up systems in place, it's not going to really work (or work as well) for you.

The *big* thing struggling practice owners are missing is their sales and conversions. Yes, selling physical therapy and converting prospective patients into full on cash paying patients is vital to your business's success. You can get all the patients you want in the door or calling you, but if you don't know how to sell or feel bad about charging them money in exchange for services, then you are going to constantly struggle to grow your business.

I recently had a strategy call with one therapist who was complaining that she didn't have enough patients and that her problem was she was only seeing 52 patients a week. When I asked her about her revenue per visit is was below $100/visit and the average number of visits was between three and five. She also told me that well over 30% of her new patients complained about the price and said that they could not afford to come see her more often.

That's not a marketing problem; that's a sales and conversions problem. This is a good problem to have and one that's easily fixed, but you can't have this problem without doing a good job marketing. My job isn't to solve your problems; my job is to give you new problems.

See, this is the problem. Business owners think they need more new patients or customers, but they are unwilling or even just unable to see what's really going on. That's where a business coach can be vital to your success.

What most cash practice owners are thinking is: "I've got to convince them to come in to see me." "I've got to somehow convince my patients that $150 ($180, $250, even $400) a visit is worth it for physical therapy." What I want you to understand here is that you are no longer selling physical therapy.

I want you to get out of the mindset of selling "physical therapy" and trying to compete with all the other traditional physical therapy clinics, massage therapists, personal trainers, etc. It is not "physical therapy" that you are offering your patients. You are selling them the transformation they really want in their life. Physical therapy is just the skillset you use to you help your patients make a radical transformation in their life.

The "transformation" is your ability to help your perfect patient go from, "I can't sleep at night because every time I roll over my back hurts and I have no energy to exercise and if I can't exercise, I'm not strong or even able to be patient with my kids," to "I now sleep easily at night, exercise five days a week and have the energy and presence I want so I can take care of my family."

That's what your patients really want. They don't want "physical therapy," i.e. hot packs, leg lifts, 10 minutes on the bike and ultrasound. They want to be able to participate in their life. Your job is to find out *why* this activity is so important to them by having a transformational and value-based conversation.

Once you are able to do this, and convert inquiries to paid in full plan of care, then it's time to go searching for your perfect patients and the proven marketing strategies in this book will go to work for you on a continual basis.

MAXIMIZING PATIENTS' VALUE

The number one thing we want to do is maximize our current patients' value. I want to talk a little bit about how to turn one to four visits into eight to ten. This is a lot simpler to tell you than it is to always put it into practice because there's a lot of dynamic things that happen. The first problem I see or hear when I talk to people is about why patients are coming in. Okay, a lot of patients will come into your clinic because they want to get out of pain. For some people, getting them out of pain is really easy. It's one to two visits. Maybe three or four. You know, "I'm out of pain. That's all I needed."

For other people, they've been in chronic pain for so long that there's nothing you're going to do to get them completely out of pain. They're looking for pain-free all the time and can even be unsatisfied patients. They won't stick around if they're unsatisfied.

Then they start judging based on now rather than the progress that was made. So, the new question I'm starting to ask and been playing with is, "What progress have you made since our last visit? What changes have you made since our last visit?" Rather than, "How are you feeling right now?" Because right now might be really shitty. It might be worse than when they started, or it might be the same, and if you get the same all the time, we have to change up the question.

Let's go back to one to four visits. This person is not having their needs or expectations met. Their expectation might be that we're going to get rid of their pain. One of the things that we can do is pre-frame the plan of care like, "This is going to take eight visits," or "This is going to take at least six visits."

When framing it in transformation terms, not pain terms, that's going to allow people to stay through their visits, rather than drop off after a few. It's almost our duty to keep our patients in our immediate ecosystem long enough to fix the real problem and make them resilient so it doesn't happen again.

One of the other ways that you can maximize the current patient value is to have patients pay ahead. The other thing we can do is to upsell them into wellness and fitness programs when they're done, and one of the ways we can do that is creating packages.

RAISING YOUR RATES

What are you worth as a healthcare professional? Think about what you paid to go to school, and what was that worth?

So, let's talk about the transformation you provide other people. What is that worth? Let's say you help someone be able to go back to work. They don't get a paycheck the week they're out of work. What is it worth to them if you help them get back to work so they can earn another $1000? They lost $1000 and are looking at losing another $1000 next week. Can you get them back in to work next week for $150, and then over the course of the next eight weeks, for $800, help them stay in their job, work comfortably and be happy at the end of the day without biting the heads off of anyone they're supervising? That's worth thousands of dollars to them.

When you raise your rates $2 or even $50, it makes a huge difference at the end of the year. If you see 1000 people in a year and charge an extra $2, that's a $2000 raise or bonus you just gave yourself.

There are people who are charging over $200 for physical therapy, but really, they're not charging $200. We're not charging $197, $175, $150 for physical therapy—we're exchanging money so that we can help a person transform their life and get back to the things that they really want to do.

When we're transforming people's lives, the limit on what we charge them is on us, not on them. If I'm trying to sell physical therapy for $150, and the guy down the street is selling the same physical therapy for a $50 copay, there's no way I'm going to win. That's the math. Come up with the number you want to get to and ask yourself, "How high do I need to raise my rates to achieve this? How many people do I need to hire to make this happen?"

The biggest mistake most cash practice owners make is setting their prices too low and failing to learn how to sell their services. When we were only charging $150/visit, we were unable to generate enough of a profit to pay a full-time physical therapist a salary that they were worth. Creating a price structure that ensures scalability and feeling comfortable selling physical therapy is exactly why I've created a new program, Ethical Influence, that all of my Platinum Mastermind students are required to complete.

Chapter 9

Online Marketing

Why do you need to market online? In order to have a highly successful business in the 21st century, you need a component that's online. It's a given.

FACEBOOK

I think the number one mistake people make trying to market their clinic or business in a Facebook post is posting something that doesn't mean anything to their audience.

Posting something that just says, "Yeah, we're great at physical therapy. Here's the exercise to fix your hip problem" doesn't provide value. You may think it is, but it's not the best strategy. You need to make it personal. Tell a personal story. Share about what the problem might be that they are experiencing and WHY it's important that they take action and do something about it today. (Of course, don't use patients' names unless you have permission!)

Facebook's algorithm changes frequently and what I'm teaching you right now may not be the best current strategy, so I'll try to stick to the basics of communication and the overall strategy of what you should be doing.

At the time of this writing, posts on your business page do not get as wide of a reach as your personal page. You need to start treating your personal page as a business profile and use Facebook and social media for business. Don't let social media use you.

Posts to your business page are still important and to get a wide reach, they are pay to play. Facebook paid advertising is one of the best and most cost-efficient paid advertising platforms you can use; however, it's not the first thing you should be doing and we'll go more into detail about it later. Before you pay for advertising you need proof that your message and offer work.

Definitely stay away from randomly just boosting posts, even if Facebook suggests it, unless you have a specific strategy. Some of your posts will be more popular than others and the more you share personal stories, the more people are going to connect with you. Track your posts and the ones that get the most likes, comments and shares are the ones you can use later to turn into blog posts or Facebook ads to build a custom audience.

One of the easiest strategies is to go live on Facebook on a regular basis, take the recording and turn it into a blog post. When you publish it, be sure you share it with a comment that includes a personal story about why it's important to read. Stories sell.

The number one mistake I see people make on Facebook, especially on their business page, is using the call to action button "Book

Now." This is a very strong commitment that you are asking people to take. You should be using the "Learn More" button, even in your Facebook Ads and website. On your Facebook business page, this button should point to your free offer, your about page or somewhere they can get more information and also see an option to schedule a consultation with you.

BLOG FEATURE

This is a great strategy too: feature a popular business owner in your town on your blog. You don't need to write a story about them, just go meet for lunch.

Build rapport by asking them questions and connecting on similar interests. At the end of your meeting ask, "This has been great. I would love to interview you for my blog. Are you interested?"

Then just email over a list of questions and publish the answers in a neat little post! You can even just send them a list of questions as a word document or online survey. Then proofread, format and publish it as a blog article.

Link back to their business and add some images. When you share it, be sure you tag the business and business owner. More often than not, the person will re-post it on their social platforms or email list too.

Pro Tip: You can use this same strategy with a local podcast that you create!

SEO

Search Engine Optimization or SEO is no longer as important as it was back in 2009 when I started, though it's still important. About 50% of our patients find us online and another huge chunk research us online before coming in. If a patient enters your name in a Google search and can't find anything about you or just even your clinic's website, then you have a *big* problem.

Your website, your personal profile and your blog should be showing up in a Google search. Just go enter "Aaron LeBauer" in both Google and YouTube and see what you find!

The easiest way to be sure a prospective patient finds you online is to not just create an "about us" page, but make a page that is about the patient, with your name in the URL or web address. Kind of like www.LeBauerPT.com/Aaron-LeBauer. This is basically a copy of my "about us" page instead of just using www.LeBauerPT.com/about.

Another good page to have is similar to www.LeBauerPT.com/Physical-Therapy-Greensboro. It could just be a mirrored page of your homepage with a different URL and slightly different copy about who you help, how you help them, some testimonials and some additional information about your perfect patient because people are going to be searching for you.

You definitely have to have a Google Business page. If you don't have a Google Business page, mark this page, stop reading and go create one right now. Go claim or create a Google My Business account and listing so you show up in Google Maps. You want to be listed in as many internet directories as possible, especially Google Maps.

Make sure you're also on Yelp. Angie's List may be a great option too. In general, you want to be on testimonial and review sites. Local one's are great.

The most important thing about search engine optimization right now is your content. Your blog and website content should be about your patients and who they are. It should be about what they want, not necessarily your qualifications and education. It should be helpful, and that's why a blog is so great because a blog updates regularly even if it's only once a month. When Google searches, it is sees there's new content and it sees that it's relevant to physical therapy or to back pain, and that's how your practice starts to show up high in listings.

SOCIAL MEDIA CONTENT EXAMPLE

What you're going to do is create one piece of original content. This is like creating a Facebook Live video or blog post. The problem with just writing a blog post is that there's not as much opportunity to use that content as there is when you start with video. Video is really powerful for a couple reasons. One, because people want to see and connect with you, and two, they like to watch TV. They like to watch video. They can learn a lot more from it. I know a lot of times I'll scroll through Facebook and I'll stop and watch a video, but if I see a long article, I'll breeze right by it.

We also want to repurpose this onto other platforms. Say you do a Facebook Live. Upload it to YouTube, cut into pieces to put on

Instagram, transcribe it and make it into a blog post. Then use it again a couple months later!

So, how do you automate it? If you go to your Facebook business page and want to set up a couple posts on there, you can schedule them out. What that means is that you sit down for a half hour one day, you write three or four posts and schedule them out for the week.

You can also use platforms that are even more robust than that and will auto-schedule to multiple social media platforms like Hootsuite. It saves you time, but the posts aren't always specific to the platform or written directly on the platform, so they're not given as high of a priority. If you can manually produce content on every platform, that's preferred by the platform. But as a business we also need to automate stuff, so mixing those together is a great strategy!

When it comes to images, let's say you have an awesome quote you said. You get an image that you can use, and you can go to Canva and put in the quote with the picture in the background. Then upload that to Instagram or Facebook with a caption explaining the quote in more depth. For photos, I recommend getting a professional photography session in different outfits so you can have content for months to come.

When we're making content, I want you guys to understand that it's important to talk about the why. It's not, "Here's the exercise that's going to fix your back pain," because a lot of people put out content like that.

A strong call to action is important to put in the copy of your posts because it's what you want people to do. Yes, we want people to call for an appointment, but people aren't going to call unless you position it as more of a "chat to see what's going on."

The call to action shouldn't always be the same. You want to mix it up. Some examples are: comment, share, call our office or fill out this form to inquire about cost and availability. There's a lot of different things you can do, but you want to take it kind of slow. We don't want to ask people like, "Hey, call me for an appointment," because they haven't met you. You want to let them feel comfortable with you first.

After posting, the goal at the very beginning is to get engagement. When you create a Facebook video, you can create an audience of the people who watch the video. Then you can create an audience of people based on those who like or engage or click on your business page posts. Engagement is also commenting below, so you want to encourage that as much as possible. The more engagement you have, the more Facebook will show your content to more people.

We've got an email list, but we've also got a list of people who engage with us on our social networks, and all those lists are important because those people may not be ready to buy right now or ready to schedule with you right now. They might like what you're saying because they've had a similar experience, but they're not ready to buy. They're going to buy soon. They might just be around the corner tomorrow or six months from now.

Another great thing to do is follow up with an invitation to join your private community. I have a LeBauer Physical Therapy business page, but also a LeBauer PT Community private group. It's a community for our patients, friends and pretty much anyone local. With some of these posts you can say, "Hey, if you want to learn more, come join our private community."

Chapter 10

Lead Generation Systems

Lastly, we're going to talk about creating a free e-book or report that provides value and converts prospects to patients. We've got to give so much info that people can't believe we have even more!

The number one principle is that you have to give to get. If I don't have something that's valuable enough, people aren't going to give me their name or email address for it. If we can give something that's super valuable that meets a need or addresses a pain point, then people are going to pony up their email and name so that they can get that information.

This is one of those things where they're voluntarily doing it, but at any time they can opt out of it. It's a private thing. I'm not sharing email addresses but providing something of value in exchange for contact information. It's a win-win.

E-BOOK CONTENT

What do we put in an e-book? Think about what people have asked you.

It's basically, "What would you advise your friend to do if they were in pain?" What you choose for your content is based on any issue that you are working in. It's also based on what are most people are looking for. What is the problem most people want to solve? For me, for most of us, it's back pain. So that's where I start. There's a whole bunch of other topics that we can do. If your practice is primarily women's health, it would be a women's health thing like, "How do you solve stress and urinary incontinence?"

When it comes to the title, you want to speak to the fears and the desires of your patients. We don't want to instill fear in them or give them false promises. We don't want to speak about, "Solve your stress and urinary incontinence with this e-book." It should be something like, "The 10 Ways to Stop Leaking While Running."

PUBLISHING

This is one of those simple things that can be kind of challenging. All you need to do is create a Microsoft Word document, then save it as a PDF. So, create your Word document. Include links, pictures and videos. What I've done is included hyperlinks to videos I find on YouTube and pictures that I've taken.

The main thing I want you to get out of this is when you make your e-book a PDF, people can't change it and then re-publish it. The PDF is always going to have your logo and name on it. One more thing: when you convert from the Word document to the

PDF, you want to make sure any hyperlinks that you included are clickable. It should do it automatically when you convert to PDF, but make sure to double-check.

I would also recommend creating an e-book cover. You can do this on your own. It doesn't have to be very fancy. I mean, it can be super plain. It can be one color with some shading or no color at all. Use stock images if you want, but the main thing is the title. Then what you can do is go on Fiverr.com and find someone to make your cover into a 2D and 3D image for your website.

OPTING IN

What you want to do is create an opt-in page on ClickFunnels or LeadPages where you can send people from your website to collect their name, email and phone number.

Because they have put in their information, these are people that are likely to become your clients. They are now highly qualified individuals. They're more likely to be your patients because they've raised their hand and said, "Hey, I'm interested. I'm interested in learning more about how to help myself or how you can help me."

I don't get a lot of calls for the free book on low back pain, but I do get a lot of phone calls. It gets people on the phone and thinking about what I'm going to do for them.

FOLLOWING UP

Let people know how often you're going to be contacting them. If you post on your blog every week say, "Hey, expect occasional emails from me and a blog post every week," or, "Expect a blog post every month and an occasional email from me with health tips." It can be more like, "I'm going to check in with you. Thanks for requesting a book. Obviously, you've had some back pain issues. I'd love to help you. Respond to this email right now and I'm going to check back in with you in a few days."

Right now, I've got a system where I've got about 30-something emails that go out every four to five days. That's a lot. I used to do once a week. Once every seven to 10 days. I did that for a long time and I'm doing it now. I've added more as I update my e-book. I've added more and I'm doing it more often with stronger calls to action. The relevant information is every couple days I'll throw out a tip on taking care of your back or why people decide not to do anything about their back.

Now if you get their phone number, you can call them. Call them within 24 hours and say, "Hey. I'm the psychical therapist that sent you the back pain e-book yesterday. How are you doing? What's going on that you're looking for help with your back pain?" Just start the conversation.

There's a lot of other ways to really work this, but making contact with people, even if they're not ready to book then, is important. Maybe even giving them some things to do on their own or answering a few questions. It can almost serve as a free 15-minute consult.

PART 3

The Entrepreneur Mindset

Before we finish up, I want to chat a little about the entrepreneur mindset.

To build a business that allows you to travel without taking a pay cut, that gives you a huge return on your investment and is something valuable enough to sell, you must create a replicable system that generates revenue over and over and over again. In a business like a clinic, that looks like a website and follow-up system that consistently generates phone calls. That is also the systems you create to serve your patients and clients day after day so that the amazing people you hire know exactly what to do to treat patients for you and to help you run the business.

Think about this: can you create an instruction manual and reliable marketing machine that runs and generates revenue for you, your family and your employees even if you are abducted by the aliens? If the answer is YES, then you have a business worth selling and one that will help you live life on your terms.

If your answer is not yet, then this final chapter is where you need to focus. What I want to leave you with is not just a formula for creating a job for yourself, but an instruction manual to grow as a person and become a ruthless business owner who values time over everything else. In this final chapter you'll learn the five principle traits of successful entrepreneurs and how to install them in yourself and so you can succeed where others have been willing to quit.

Chapter 11

Entrepreneur Mindset

INVESTING

Expenses are things that are expensive or expensive to some people. Investments are things that you spend money or time on and down the road they return a greater value.

If you're in the stock market, right now the chance that you will have a good return on your investment in 15, 20 years is good, because historically the stock market has always gone up. This is not a book about the stock market. This is a book about your business, and your business can go up, it can stay still, and it can go away. When choosing where to spend your time and money, entrepreneurs look at every transaction considering, "Am I going to get a return on my investment for the time or money that I spend?"

New business owners and people that struggle as entrepreneurs judge these same transactions as expensive. Entrepreneurs look at their actions, time and transactions as investments they can get a return on.

Being better at business requires learning about business, not just gaining more knowledge treating patients. Investing in your business knowledge, reading books, taking courses and working with coaches and mentors is how you ensure your success and sharpen your business skills.

BMW's are expensive. Learning better business skills and working with a business coach is a great investment.

CREATING SYSTEMS

Entrepreneurs also create systems. A system is something as easy as a video that teaches you how to do a task, or a checklist that walks you through the steps. It can be an email automation that takes people from point A to point B. It can be just a rule that you've set up that every time someone calls, or every time someone becomes a patient, you send them a "Thank You" card. That's a system. It's something that's expected to happen over and over again.

Your systems run your business and the people you hire run the systems. Think ahead, "Okay, in five years I know where I want to be so right now, as I set this up, I need to write it down so that the next person can do it." While you have more time now, it's a great time to create the systems versus waiting until you're really busy and go, "Shit. I need to hire an assistant. I didn't write any of this stuff down and I've got 26 patients a week and I don't have time to do anything else, and I have to do this," which is kind of what happened to me.

Successful entrepreneurs don't do everything themselves. Check the ego at the door. That includes finding someone to help you, who's already done it, to show you the shortcut to getting it done.

Where you can be spending your time selling or treating a patient, if someone else is there to change the rooms, clean, answer the phone and greet patients, it makes your time more efficient.

It's all about buying your time back.

THE MONEY MINDSET

The money mindset is important and it's a difficult one for everyone because a lot of people are brought up thinking about money in different ways. A lot of times our parents are not business owners or entrepreneurs. My dad for example is not an entrepreneur. He is a Cardiologist who was in business for himself. When I told him that I paid $25,000 to go work with a coach, fly out to California and spend four hours with him, he looked at me like I was crazy.

He just didn't get it. He was a physician that was thrown into business ownership because of how physicians operated back in the day. They just were all individual entities that formed partnerships and today are largely employed by hospital systems. Many of these physician business owners made poor business decisions because their drive and goal was just to serve patients who were sick.

A lot of people grow up in a "money is bad" mindset and when money's bad, when things are expensive, you may not want to make money. That leads to people having trouble getting off the ground and moving into business where they are asking $150-250 a visit because they say, "I wouldn't even pay that myself!"

The other thing about money is that most people don't think big enough. I certainly didn't. I didn't have a reference point for how much I needed or how much what I wanted in life. Many therapists

I speak with just, "want to earn four thousand dollars a month so that I can replace my PRN job."

The best way to know how much you need is to work backwards. Think about how much you need to earn each year to get what you want and to save and invest enough to have it once you move into the next stage of life, whether it's a traditional "retirement" or a new venture.

Once you know this amount, I want you to think about this: if you had twice or even ten times that amount, what more could you do for your community with the extra income? How else could you support your community, the people in your life or the causes you believe in? What can you create that will leave a legacy if you think bigger? Because if you're not thinking big enough, you cannot create that.

I want to generate enough income so I get to a point in my life where I feel like it's hard to give enough away. In Judaism, Tikun Olam is the concept of striving to improve the world in which we live. Certainly working to ensure people know their options and get physical therapy to avoid unnecessary surgery works towards this principle and being financially able to support organizations that align with my beliefs is another important step in leaving this place better for my children and others who will dwell here long after I'm gone.

VALUE TIME

Time is your most valuable asset. It's the one thing that you cannot get more of. We are all going to die. You can, however, maximize your time and spend more of your time doing what you want and enjoy.

As an entrepreneur, you should always be considering, "Can someone else do this just as well as me, or at least 80% as good, for less?" If you can hire someone for $15/hour to make phone calls, change over treatment rooms and greet patients so that you can treat patients for $250/hour, don't hesitate.

I was recently on the phone with one of my Platinum Mastermind students who was asking about taking out a loan so she can bring on her assistant full time. She asked me if I thought it was a good idea. Instead of just saying "yes," my response was, "Do you think if you hire her, you'll have an extra 20 hours a week to develop your programs and seminars, treat more patients and generate more than $20/hour?" Her answer was a resounding "YES!"

So, if you can buy back your time by hiring a great employee, stop being afraid and go for it. A personable, bright and intelligent employee with robust systems to follow will be worth much more to your business and help you achieve your goals. Hiring employees is not expensive—it is actually the least expensive way for you to buy more time in your day to focus on the work that means the most to you.

TAKING ACTION

Action trumps perfection 100% of the time and if you make a decision that turns out to be the wrong one, you just fix it. You course correct. You go back and adjust. When people get into a place where they can't make a decision and get caught up in the "paralysis by analysis," they fail to move forward. They don't grow and they don't succeed.

It is not in the decision-making process where you should be spending the majority of your time. Make a choice, trust your gut and go for it. Failure is not an option. There are only opportunities to learn and grow.

That's what I've done working with my coaches. I pay them to help me decide what action to take and to know what systems to put into place because they are exactly where I want to be. They make a recommendation, I get it done and generally get a huge return on my investment.

Make a list, use a daily planner, prioritize your tasks and focus on the tasks that are going to move the needle for you. Most successful entrepreneurs have an idea of what tomorrow is going to be. It's planned out, non-negotiable time blocked out on their calendar. You can even start by making one day of the week an administrative day where you work on your business and get it done!

80% IS GOOD ENOUGH

In school, you were expected to get straight "A's" and strive for 100%. Perfection is a business killer! Your e-book, website, promotion, etc. will never be perfect so stop waiting for it to be "just right" before you launch. All you are doing is letting excuses get in your way of forward progress and becoming successful.

In business, 80% is good enough. Take this book for example. I'm sure you've found a few typos and absolutely it could be even better, but waiting another year or more to get it perfect and "just right" would have kept it out of your hands longer.

I've worked with so many people who are stuck, stalled out and fail to make the forward progress in their business they expected. The number one reason? They fail to take action. The number one excuse I hear from these people is that they "were not ready" and that their product/promotion/idea wasn't finished.

Who cares? I don't. Neither do your customers who just want your help.

As long as your idea, product or strategy is "good enough," go ahead and put it in play. Publish your website and get it out there in front of your target customer. The sooner you do this, the sooner you'll achieve massive results and know if your time, energy and ideas were the right ones.

If it's not a winning combination, you'll know before you put even more time into it. Likely, it's good and will resonate with people and you'll get more and bigger results sooner, maybe even with less effort than you anticipated. You'll always have an opportunity to go back and refine your product and message, even tweak it to respond to the needs and feedback of your customers.

Now that you are done with school, you no longer need to get straight "A's." You didn't need an A on your licensure exam; you only needed to pass. In business, you just need to shoot for a passing grade and then move on to the next big task that's going to move the needle for your business.

Get over it and start taking massive action. You only get paid when it's done! 80% is good enough.

Aaron LeBauer

WHAT'S NEXT?

I would hope that at this point it's no longer a question of, "Will a cash-based physical therapy practice will work?" It's only a question of, "When will you decide to start one yourself?"

Once you start a cash practice or any business, you have built yourself a job. If you want to truly create the CashPT® Lifestyle and live life on your terms, you need to plan on hiring staff and scaling your business. When you do this, you truly become an entrepreneur.

One of my big life goals is to have location and time freedom by the time my girls graduate high school and go off to college. What this means is that I can go live in San Diego, Boulder or even the coast of Spain for a month or more just because I want to. I'll probably do that and work while I'm there because I love it. I technically already have this, except we don't want to take our kids out of their school and away from their friends.

You may have different goals and dreams. But whatever those are, the worst possible outcome for you would be to just shut down your business because you built it all about you.

Last year I had a cash practice owner call me asking to help her sell her business because she was moving out of town. Not only was she moving in less than a month, she had built the whole thing around her personal treatments and one-on-one time with patients. She didn't have an email list or an automated system of generating patients. She had nothing to sell.

Build your business to sell, then when the time comes, you can just hire someone to run it for you if you're not ready to sell.

Thanks for reading! Here is what to do next…

Check out the Free resources and trainings in the back of this book! →

To Your Success!

Free Training

If you liked this book and you want to start (or recently started) a cash-based practice, I'm sure you'll love this Free training on…

How to Create a Cash-Based Physical Therapy Practice Even When Patients THINK They Need to Use Their Insurance!

Here's what you'll learn on this webinar:

- A Step-By-Step Template to start a cash-based practice from scratch
- Seamlessly transition your "in-network" practice to 100% Cash-Based
- Easily get patients to contact you directly to schedule an evaluation
- Freedom **in Practice!** Treat your patients as YOU decide they should be treated, not insurance companies. Set your own schedule. Spend more time with your family
- The Proven Way to Build Your Cash-Based Practice and Fill It with Patients!

Secure your spot in this exclusive training now!

Go To → **AaronLeBauer.com/Free-Webinar**

If you're just getting started or are less than one year in, The CashPT® Blueprint is going to be critical to your success.

I've jam packed everything into this proven step-by-step training program to ensure your success!

Here's what you'll get:

- 9 Module Online Training Course
- Premium Video Training
- Downloadable MP3 Recordings & PDF Handouts
- Exclusive Resources

FREE Bonuses included with this training:

- The CashPT® Toolkit
- The MobilePT Academy
- The GymPT® Formula
- Google Apps/G Suite for Your EMR
- Medicare & Cash Pay Physical Therapy Training
- Lifetime Membership: Aaron's Physical Therapy Business Ignition Group

Over 500 people have already graduated from this program and built successful cash-based practices, so be sure you don't miss out!

Learn More Here → **AaronLeBauer.com/Blueprint**

Free Masterclass

If you already own a physical therapy business and want to learn how to grow and scale so you can have the greatest impact possible, then you need to join this Free Masterclass where you'll learn…

The 7 Most Critical Systems to Create Time & Freedom for Any Physical Therapy Business Owner!

In this Masterclass, you'll discover:

- How to put your clinic on autopilot!
- The easy way to get new cash paying patients that does not require you to ask for referrals
- The key marketing strategies you need to start growing your physical therapy business
- How to get new patients without buying expensive ads in the newspaper or local magazines
- How to leverage your time and resources to build systems in your business that give you the freedom to create a massive impact in your community and **transform** your life!

Claim your spot today!

Register Here → **AaronLeBauer.com/7-Systems**

THE CASHPT® PLATINUM MASTERMIND

If you're already a business owner but not generating the revenue you think you deserve or have the time freedom you want, and would like to grow and scale your business in the fastest amount of time possible, then you may be a great fit for The CashPT® Platinum Mastermind coaching group.

WARNING: The CashPT® Platinum Mastermind program is NOT for everyone. This is for ambitious action takers only who are ready to apply the proven systems and implement the profit boosting strategies to take your business to massive success. If you are not willing to do the work, DO NOT apply for this coaching program – you will not be accepted.

Here's what you'll get as a part of this exclusive coaching group:

- Access to all of my products, including my flagship courses: The CashPT® Blueprint, The CashPT® Marketing System and The Physical Therapy Business University
- An invitation to three in-person live events per year
- Access to three live coaching calls per month
- Membership to our private Platinum Mastermind community where everyone shares their biggest business wins and where you'll get motivation and support to achieve massive success!

This is your opportunity to 10X Your Marketing, 10X Your Action, 10X Your Thinking, 10X Your Income and 10X Your Impact in 12 Months or Less!

Learn all the details and submit your application
→ **AaronLeBauer.com/Mastermind**

Appendix

The CashPT® Checklist

Business Set-Up

- State License to practice Physical Therapy
- City and/or State Business License (healing art or art of healing license)
- Business Entity Status: LLC, PLLC, S-Corp, etc.
- Business Name or DBA
- Liability Insurance
- Individual & General Liability (slip & fall) for your physical location
- Permits for signage
- Building inspection

Location & Operations

- Payment Policy
- Cancellation & No-Show Policy
- Rental or Sublease Agreement
- If no physical location – Mailing Address
- P.O. Box vs. Your Home Address
- Telephone Number & Service Installation

- Internet Service Installation
- Business Checking & Savings Account
- Order Checks
- Computer, Tablet, and/or Smartphone
- Credit Card Processing
- Documentation System
- EMR or Handwritten SOAPS
- Informed Consent
- Treatment, Photographs, Communication
- Privacy Statement
- Medicare Beneficiary Consent

Marketing

- Business Logo
- Website/Blog
- Google Local Listing
- Yahoo/Bing Local Listings
- Local *Non-Paid* Phone Book Listing
- Business Cards
- Email Marketing & Auto-Responder Service
- List of contacts (including phone #'s & email addresses) in your community
- Fitness Pros, Yoga/Pilates Instructors, Personal Trainers, Faith Community, Physicians, etc.

Download this exact checklist for Free here →
AaronLeBauer.com/Checklist

To check out the companies I recommend and to get some discounts to use them in your business, go here → **AaronLeBauer.com/Resources**

Daily Success Checklist

Review Your Why

- o Who are you contributing to? Who are you doing this for? Family? Greatest patient transformations?

Start Your Day Right

- o Move every day and exercise. Maintain a movement practice, even if it's just 10 minutes when you get to the office. Workout, go to yoga, or do some air squats at the office.
- o We can't expect our patients to do something we're unwilling to do ourselves.

Review & Prioritize Your Action Steps

- o What are you implementing this week? What did you learn recently that you need to put into action?
- o What's the #1 thing you need to accomplish? Take it 1 step at a time to reduce feeling overwhelmed.

Review Your Goals

- o Revisit your 1, 5- and 10-year goals
- o Write down the progress you have made towards your goals.
- o Write down what you need to do today and what you need to work on to make progress this week.

Review Your Schedule

- o Look at your schedule today and for this week.
- o Where can you maximize your time?
- o Time block your days and week.

Set Aside At Least 1 Day Each Week to Work "ON" Your Business

- o Set aside at least 1 full day a week to work "ON" your business. It's much more efficient to treat patients Monday, Wednesdays & Fridays and build your business Tuesdays and Thursdays.

Ask Questions, Share and Pay It Forward

- o Share Your Success, Ask Your Questions and Pay It Forward in the Facebook Group. You will get faster results if you know what's already working for others and deepen your knowledge as you pass it on.
- o Be sure you invest time and finances for the coaching you need to enhance your learning, growth and speed of success. You are not alone on this journey. We are here for you to lean on.

Review Your Lead Tags

- Where are your patients finding you?
- Who is your #1 referral partner this week? Month? Year?

Review Your Conversion Rate

- How many people are calling/inquiring vs scheduling an evaluation?
- What are your numbers for last week? This week? Next week?

Review Your Sales & Marketing Strategies

- What's working? What is not?
- Where can you improve your message? Your target audience? Your Leads? Your offer?

Review Your Systems

- Double check your email sequences, systems, scripts, etc.
- Do they need updating? Are you testing them? Subscribe yourself to one of your lists or e-books.

Optimize, automate, then outsource, everything in your business that is a "fire" that you have to put out, an emergency that you have to handle, or anything else that drains your energy.

"Do You Take My Insurance?" Call Script

You: *"Hello, this is LeBauer Physical Therapy."*

Patient: *"Hello. Do You Take My Insurance?"*

Take a deep breath.

Before you answer, what would happen if you just said "no"? Would they hang up? First, let's get this conversation started off on the right foot. Introduce yourself and begin to engage a conversation.

"This is Dr. LeBauer speaking. Whom am I speaking with?"

Try these engaging questions:

"Hello Mrs. Jones, how did you hear about our practice?"

"What's going on that you are looking for physical therapy?"

"Where does it hurt?"

"How long have you experienced this problem? What have you tried in the past to decrease the pain?"

"What are you unable to do because of this problem? Or, what are you unable to do as well as you would like because of this problem?"

We are trying to figure out what their motivation is for calling us now vs. 3 months ago. Sometimes they need some prodding.

"Has something changed recently that you've now decided you need to look for a different solution or alternative?"

Or

"Why are you calling us today vs 3 months ago when this 1st became a problem?"

Reassure them that they've called the right place and let them know that you can help.

"We can definitely help you with _____ and we help people with this type of problem all the time."

We want to know what they are expecting. This helps frame how we describe what we are providing so they can better understand how we are different than their other options.

"What is your understanding of what physical therapy can do for you?

"Mrs. Jones, imagine if we were having this conversation again in 3 months, even a year from now. Looking back over that time, what has to happen for you to feel happy with your progress and that working with us was the best decision you ever made?" ?"

"This is something we see all the time in our clinic and I'm quite sure we can help you make some significant changes in what you are able to do.

Is it OK with you if I describe a bit about what we do here at LeBauer Physical Therapy?"

"Does this sound like what you are looking for?"

Usually the patient will also answer "yes."

What question do you have for me that I can answer which will help you make a decision about working with us?"

"Can we go ahead and get you scheduled for an evaluation with Dr. _____ or do you feel like you would benefit from one of our Free Total Body Diagnostic exams before moving forward with an evaluation?"

Thank You Note Script

Dear (Patient's First Name),

Welcome to the LeBauer family!

It was great working with you during your visit to our clinic today.

Thank you for giving us the opportunity to help you stay fit, healthy and mobile without pain medications, injections or surgery.

We are committed to doing everything we can to help you (Insert patients #1 goal here).

You're in good hands.

Sincerely,

Dr. Aaron LeBauer
LeBauer Physical Therapy

Patient Re-Activation Email Script

Subject Line: *Checking in...*

Hi %FIRSTNAME%,

I just wanted to send you a quick message and check in with you.

How are you doing since our last appointment?

How have you been feeling?

Do you have any questions for me or is there anything else I can do for you?

Thanks,

Dr. Your Last Name

List of Local Fitness and Health Professionals to Contact

Name	Phone #	Website
1		
2		
3		
4		
5		
6		
7		
8		
9		
10		

Sample Superbill

LeBauer Physical Therapy LLC
319 Smyres Pl
Greensboro, NC 27403

Sales Receipt

Sold To
Aaron LeBauer
319 Smyres Place
Greensboro, NC 27403

Date of Service 4/2/2013
Sale # 2863

Check #
Payment Method

Your Next Appointment is:

Place of Service: OFFICE CODE #11

ICD-9/Diagnosis Codes:

724.2, 355.0

Description	Qty	Rate	Amount
97001 Physical Therapy Evaluation	1		0.00
97140 Manual Therapy/Myofascial Release	1		0.00
97110 Therapeutic Exercise	1		0.00

Aaron LeBauer PT, DPT, LMBT

Patient Paid Balance in Full
LeBauer Physical Therapy, LLC is NOT an insurance provider for this claim.
Please provide payment directly to the patient.

Subtotal $0.00
Sales Tax (6.75%) $0.00
Total

LeBauer Physical Therapy LLC   EIN #
@gmail.com
www.LeBauerPT.com

NC License #
336-
336-

Notes

Acknowledgements

A special thanks to…

The CashPT® Nation. That's you. The legion of physical therapists and healthcare providers who, no matter what, are dedicated to doing what's right for patients, even if the healthcare system and insurance companies want to treat them like a number.

To my beautiful wife and kids, Andra, Sophie and Elena, for their unconditional support, love and affection. I couldn't have done this without you.

To the rest of my family: my Aunts, Uncles, Grandparents, cousins and brothers. Without your input, influence and legacy, the impact on our communities wouldn't be the same.

To my good friend and success partner, Greg Todd, for always having my back and helping me level up!

To my business coaches—Allen, Scott, Jon, Lewis and Bedros—for their inspiration, mentorship and without whom I'd still be trying to reinvent the wheel.

To Brenna, my amazing content specialist (and young adult author in her own right) for editing this 1st edition and organizing all the ideas and thoughts flowing out of my head!

About the Author

Aaron LeBauer is the host of The CashPT® Lunch Hour Podcast, The CashPT® Nation Facebook group and has helped 1000's of passionate physical therapists create and grow successful businesses without relying on insurance.

He is a Doctor of Physical Therapy, Certified Massage Therapist, and Baptiste Inspired Yoga Teacher. He opened LeBauer Physical Therapy, a 100% cash-based physical therapy practice in Greensboro, NC with his wife Andra the day after he graduated from PT school in 2008. After seeing 43 patients in one day as a PT student, he knew he could not treat patients effectively in the insurance model.

LeBauer started his 100% cash practice so he could treat patients as unique individuals and without influence by insurance reimbursement and has inspired 1000's of others to do the same even when physicians, professors, and other physical therapists think it's a crazy idea, unethical or will simply not work.

He is on a mission to save 100 million people from unnecessary surgery by helping other passionate therapists succeed in business and learn how to market directly to patients.

Follow Aaron on his journey here → AaronLeBauer.com